CONSHOHOCKEN AND
WEST CONSHOHOCKEN SPORTS

Basketball has always been a popular sport at the Fellowship House. By the mid-1950s and through the 1960s, different leagues were developed according to age. In more recent years, the Fellowship House has given way to organized basketball as the Catholic Youth Organization and area biddy leagues have filled that void, but all of these organizations still use the Fellowship House for all their practices and games.

On the front cover: George Snear, No. 70, and Stan Sachaczenski (better known as "Sacs"), No. 63, pose for a photograph before a game in the fall of 1945. (Courtesy of George Snear.)

On the back cover: Standing in the back on the right is manager Art "Tuti" Andrey, and on the left is coach Burr Robbins. Players on the 1969 Blue Jays Little League team include, in no special order, William Schwegel, John Walker, George McMonagle, Dennis Tolan, Joe Carlin, Art Andrey, John Borrelli, Richard Tobin, Pat Ferris, John DeMedio, Ernie Martinelli, Kevin Brown, John Maresca, Jim Cushwa, and Richard Robbins. (Author's collection.)

Cover background: See page 76. (Author's collection.)

CONSHOHOCKEN AND
WEST CONSHOHOCKEN SPORTS

Jack Coll

ARCADIA
PUBLISHING

Copyright © 2009 by Jack Coll
ISBN 978-0-7385-6542-2

Published by Arcadia Publishing
Charleston SC, Chicago IL, Portsmouth NH, San Francisco CA

Printed in the United States of America

Library of Congress Control Number: 2008941495

For all general information contact Arcadia Publishing at:
Telephone 843-853-2070
Fax 843-853-0044
E-mail sales@arcadiapublishing.com
For customer service and orders:
Toll-Free 1-888-313-2665

Visit us on the Internet at www.arcadiapublishing.com

This book is dedicated to every athlete who ever

put on a uniform representing the great boroughs of

Conshohocken and West Conshohocken.

CONTENTS

ACKNOWLEDGMENTS

In the late 1970s, I was fortunate enough to meet John "Chick" McCarter, a great local sports historian. Over the next decade, Chick provided me with hundreds of sports photographs, along with the stories that made them fascinating. Throughout the years, dozens of Conshohocken residents have shared their precious family photographs with me, pictures of their fathers and grandfathers playing sports in the town or representing the town. George Snear is one such resident whom I would like to thank for his input into creating this wonderful sports book and for providing me with a number of photographs.

Many of the photographs taken in the 1920s and 1930s were taken by Hagar's Studios once located on Fayette Street and Bussa Studios from Norristown. The Conshohocken Library is a great source for local historical information. Located at Third Avenue and Fayette Street, the Conshohocken Library has a complete record on microfilm of the *Conshohocken Recorder* newspaper starting in the 1870s. The Historical Society of Montgomery County, located on Dekalb Pike in Norristown, is also an information source for all your historical research needs. Other photographs appearing in this book came courtesy of Patricia Barr, the Conshohocken Fellowship House, the Conshohocken Historical Society, Temple University Urban Archives, Pete Crippen, Paula Schwartz Reed, Angie Palermo, Ange D'Amico, Connie Traill Touhey, Patty Paul, Florence Cherry Barolt, Jack Frost, and the Norristown Times Herald. I would also like to acknowledge the late Walt Hannum, who wrote for the *Conshohocken Recorder* for more than half a century. Walt loved sports, and I am grateful for the factual sports articles he was able to record in the newspaper. Unless otherwise noted, all images appearing in the book are now within my personal collection.

INTRODUCTION

To understand Conshohocken's and West Conshohocken's sports history, one must first understand the towns' histories and the towns' residents. These two Pennsylvania boroughs are divided by the Schuylkill River located just 15 miles from Center City Philadelphia. In the 1830s, the Schuylkill River and the canal that ran on Conshohocken's side of the river attracted steel and cotton mills. These mills required employees who lived in the villages on each side of the river. By 1900, nearly 10,000 jobs were available along the riverfront and in the hills of both communities. Without radios, television sets, or shopping malls, sports became the great American outlet.

Organized baseball came to Conshohocken in the mid-1880s, that first ball club being called the Nerve of Conshohocken. Playing for the Nerve were pitcher Johnny Heffelfinger and former West Conshohocken lawman Horace Cassey. Conshohocken's first policeman, Jack Harrold (later the owner of Harrold's Hotel), also played for the Nerve. Conshohocken's second baseball team, called the Aerials, was a very good baseball team led by West Conshohocken resident Ed Harrison, who later owned and operated a carpet mill on the west side, once located at the former site of the Four Falls Inn. These early teams played their games at the Meadow, located along the river at Washington and Cherry Streets, an open field on the upper part of Ford Street in the west borough, and on Mud Hollow Field in Gulph Mills.

Since that first baseball team formed in the 1880s, a long list of great baseball players have emerged from both boroughs, including Roy Ellam, Perk Smith, Ira "Whitey" Mellor, Chot Wood, Paul Burton, Leo Redmond, Bill "Parry" Murphy, Rob Reed, and Dave Traill, just to name a few.

The Conshohockens were known throughout the state of Pennsylvania for their winning ways in football. Conshohocken's first organized football team was formed in 1893. By 1905, interest slipped in the sport in Conshohocken, but in 1903, the West Conshohocken Reliance Club formed a football team. Over the next 10 years, West Conshohocken Reliance teams won three Schuylkill Valley League championships.

But in 1914, a number of the Reliance team players crossed the river to the Conshohocken side and formed what became known as the Conshohocken professional team. Over the next 10 years, Conshohocken made its mark on professional football, winning a number of championships, and from 1914 to 1916, the team rolled off a 26-0 three-year record. These early teams would draw between 6,000 and 8,000 fans per game, and when Conshohocken played away games, the town would charter private trains to follow the team to opposing fields. In 1919, the undefeated Conshohocken professional football team was declared Eastern Seaboard League champions. Years later, the Pro Football Hall of Fame honored the 1919 team, hanging a team photograph in the hall, which is located in Canton, Ohio.

In the 1920s and 1930s, football was so popular in Conshohocken that more than 10 different teams would be playing football during the same season. Perhaps the highlight of the Conshohocken communities came from 1944 to 1966 when Conshohocken High School and St. Matthew's High School would meet for the annual Thanksgiving Day football game. More than 6,000 fans would gather at the Conshohocken Community Field for the annual event.

The first organized basketball team in Conshohocken was in 1895 and called the Conshohocken Pioneers. That team was led by Bob Crawford, Billy Bennett, and William Neville. By 1904–1905, Neville managed the Conshohocken basketball team to become the first world champions of professional basketball. A photograph of the 1904–1905 team hangs in the Naismith Memorial Basketball Hall of Fame.

The annual Albert C. Donofrio Basketball Tournament is played for two weeks every year at the Conshohocken Fellowship House. The tournament at one time invited the best high school basketball players from five different states to compete. Big-time players who competed at the Fellowship House reads like a who's who in the National Basketball Association: Earl "the Pearl" Monroe, Joe Bryant, Rasheed Wallace, Aaron McKie, John Salmons, Gene Banks, Fred Carter, Kobe Bryant, and Jameer Nelson, along with dozens of others. Let's not forget the baseball and football alum that have also played basketball at the tournament like John Pergine, Reggie Jackson, Steve Bono, and Brad Scioli.

The Donofrio tournament started in 1960 and was called the Conshohocken Teenage Basketball Classic; the tournament was played on the outdoor basketball courts. Albert C. Donofrio was the Fellowship House director and started the league to keep kids off the street between the basketball and baseball seasons. The tournament quickly grew, and by 1962, the tournament moved inside the Fellowship House and the amount of teams were expanded. Over the next 15 years, Division I college coaches from all over the country started showing up at the tournament to scout untapped talent, and players were getting signed to major colleges on the court after playing a game. On July 4, 1976, Donofrio passed away, and in the fall of 1976, the tournament was renamed the Albert C. Donofrio Basketball Tournament and is stronger than ever.

Myron Scott was a photographer for a Dayton, Ohio, newspaper in 1933 when he received an assignment to photograph two boys in homemade soap box racing cars. Scott realized the potential for an annual event with photo opportunities. In 1934, the first annual All-American Soap Box Derby race for boys was held in Dayton; the following year, the race was moved to Akron, Ohio, because of its central location and hilly terrain, and it has been held in Akron every year since.

In 1938, Conshohocken ran its first annual soap box derby race on Spring Mill Avenue, and Walt Cherry beat 75 other contestants in front of more than 5,000 spectators.

The event was such a success that another race was held in 1939 with the same result, as Walt Cherry won for a second time, again in front of more than 5,000 residents. Talk of war interrupted the annual race, and it did not return until 1951 when Dave McQuirns won what was called the Push Mobile Race on Fayette Street.

In 1952, thanks to the efforts of Moore's Chevrolet located on upper Fayette Street, Conshohocken's soap box derby became sanctioned with the All-American race based in Akron. Conshohocken continues to send three champions per year to Akron to represent the town in the All-American event.

Conshohocken Little League baseball was founded in the spring of 1955. A group of residents who were members of the Conshohocken Bocce Club (CBC), led by Emidio Cardamone who proposed the idea, reasoned that a Little League would provide wholesome fun and competitive alternatives to hanging on the street corners during the summer months. With the help of Francis Carr, Ange D'Amico, David Hayes, Elmer Munro, and several others, the foundation of the league was laid down at the CBC on a cold spring night all those years ago.

Four teams were formed consisting of 48 players, and games were played on Saturday mornings at Rossi Memorial Field, located behind the CBC on West Third Avenue.

The following year, more than 300 children turned out for tryouts. Within four years, a new ballpark was built at Mary Jane Sutcliffe Park, and the league was expanded to six teams.

By the 1960s, residents like John Cassinelli, Ange D'Amico, Art "Tuti" Andrey, Norman Santangelo, Ray and Phil Gravinese, and many other residents who coached, managed or umpired helped make Conshohocken one of the most successful programs in the district. By the 1990s, more than 450 children were playing Little League baseball in Conshohocken on five ball fields at Mary Jane Sutcliffe Park. Little League Inc. still remains the largest youth sports program in the world with nearly three million children, boys and girls, playing worldwide.

Conshohocken youth football was founded in 1961 with two weight classes. Over the years, the football program has undergone many changes and has participated in four different leagues, including the Pop Warner League and the Keystone State League. Conshohocken's youth football today, known as the Golden Bears, still has a strong league, adding to its long list of championship teams every year.

The Conshohocken Fellowship House is unique to Conshohocken. The Fellowship House known as the "Fel," was built as a youth center back in 1953. In the early days, sports for boys and girls were the main activity, including baseball, basketball, kickball, volleyball, badminton, golf, ice-skating, and several other sporting activities. Programs and playtime were also a big part of the schedule, including hat-making classes, pet grooming, and etiquette classes for girls.

In the mid-1970s, the Conshohocken Sports Hall of Fame was founded, and the Fellowship House was home for the hall of fame. For more than half a century, the Fellowship House has been a safe haven for thousands of Conshohocken children who have taken part in hundreds of programs.

Perhaps the very best part of *Conshohocken and West Conshohocken Sports* is the miscellaneous chapter. Conshohocken and West Conshohocken had world-class boxers back in the 1920s and 1930s, including Midget Fox, Johnny Craven, Bunny Blake, and Joey Hatfield. The boroughs have had world champion trapshooters, swimmers, and rowers. The CBC has produced championship bocce teams since 1929, the Conshohocken A Field has hosted world championship benefit wrestling matches, not to mention the communities interest in golf and ice-skating.

Another big part of sports is the cheerleaders, bands, and spectators. *Conshohocken and West Conshohocken Sports* has all that and more. This amount of local sports photographs has never been assembled for any project until now.

Joanne Wright Iverson graduated from St. Matthew's High School in 1957, and at her 1985 induction into the Conshohocken Sports Hall of Fame, Iverson was called one of America's famous women athletes. Iverson won the U.S. singles sculling championship in 1960–1963 and was the first coach of women's rowing for the University of Pennsylvania in 1972. She was manager of the first U.S. women's rowing team at the world championships in Moscow in 1973 and appointed to the U.S. Olympic Sports Commission by Pres. Gerald Ford in 1976. In 1976, she also managed the U.S. Olympic team for women's rowing in Montreal.

1

FOOTBALL

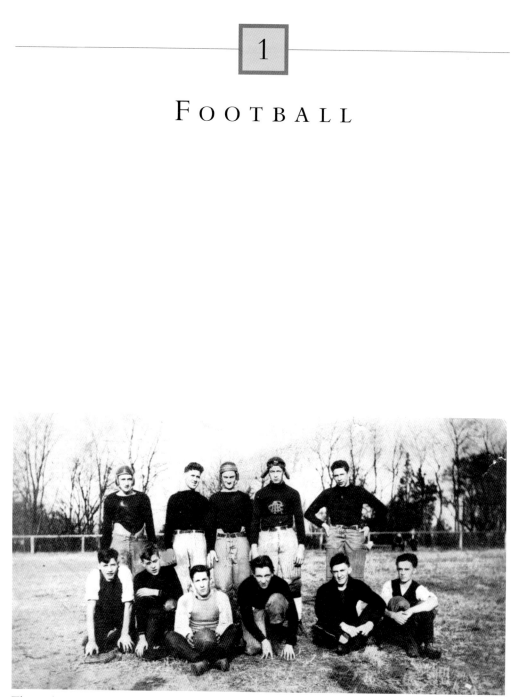

The early Conshohocken Reliance Club football teams always fielded good teams. The club was a sports organization with charters in both boroughs, and quality players could be found in the many mills along the river. This mid-1920s Conshohocken Reliance Club team includes Bill Hastings, Sol Laverty, Charles Kriebel, Sam Hiltner, John Gray, and the two Irwin brothers, Jones and Whiton.

Conshohocken's first football team was organized in 1893. The team, sponsored by the YMCA, was called the Ironmen. Members of that first team include Sam Wright, Ben Cressman, Charles Herron, Fred and Arthur Clark (sons of Charles Heber Clark, nationally known author), Eugene and Bud Beaver (sons of David Beaver, a Civil War surgeon with his home and office at the corner of East Fourth Avenue and Harry Street for many years), Alan Caine, George Lukens, and Louis and Max Vielhaber.

Conshohocken's football team from 1895 played teams like Norristown, Swedeland, and Phoenixville. Most of the players on this team played together for five or six years until a number of the players went on to play with other teams. Bob Crawford (holding the football) later owned and managed the great Conshohocken professional teams from 1914 to 1922. Crawford was also a basketball standout in the early years of sports in Conshohocken and owned Crawford's Cigar Store.

The West Conshohocken Reliance Club had one of the strongest football teams in eastern Pennsylvania from 1904 to 1913, winning three Schuylkill Valley championships. Members of the 1906 team pictured are, from left to right, (first row) Jimmy Gordon and Ed Finney; (second row) Ed Egan, Harry Ellam, Ambrose Hyde, and Ed Cooper; (third row) Ed Hyde, unidentified, Roy Ramey, Harry Reynolds, Jim Boyle, John Egan, and Walter Cook.

The West Conshohocken Reliance Club football teams for more than a decade brought out the most talented athletes of the borough, including members of this 1907 Schuylkill Valley championship team. Members of the squad included Howard Armitage, John Gordon, Hoppy Pennington, Ed Egan, John Egan, Harry Reynolds, Harry Ellam, Jim Boyle, Ed Hyde, Ed Cooper, Ed Finney, and Walter Cooper.

The 1908 West Conshohocken Reliance Club football team celebrated a championship over the Norristown JAC. Members of the 1908 championship team include, from left to right, the following: (first row) Finney, Armitage, Egan, Egan, and unidentified; (second row) Pennington, Armitage, Boyle, and Bishop; (third row) Adams, unidentified, Ellam, Hyde, Hyde, and Ellam.

In 1910, a group of St. Matthew's High School students formed a football team led by senior Art Kehoe. They challenged a group of football players from Conshohocken High School to play two games. Pictured are, from left to right, the following: (first row) Jesse Dewees, Francis Hoey, and Charles Murray; (second row) Bill Kindregan, James Darby, Joseph Kindregan, Lester Gimber, and John Dempsey; (third row) James Gorman, John "Pud" Johnson, Dan O'Connor, John McGonigal, Louis Kelly, John Hoey, Thomas Levering, and Thomas Kehoe.

FOOTBALL

The 1911 West Conshohocken Reliance Club team played most of its games behind the Mingo Hotel, once located in the 1000 block of Ford Street. The field is now a part of the Blue Route ramp. All the players are not identified, but those identified include the following: Ed Egan, John Egan, Jim Boyle, Howard Armitage, Olden Bishop, Chitzer Armitage, John Shade, Pierce Noble, ? Kindregan, Harry Ellam, Bill Lukens, Ed Hyde, and Pick Campbell.

In 1914, Conshohocken fielded the first professional football team in the borough's history. The team posted a 12-0 undefeated season, beating teams like the 1913 Frankford Athletic Association, said to be the best independent team in existence. Members of the championship Conshohocken team include, from left to right, the following: (first row) O'Donnell, Campbell, O'Donnell, Pennington, Riggs, and Hopkins (referee); (second row) "Big Phil," Carter, Bergey, Kriebel, King, Crawford, Armitage, Schall, Pownall, Noble, Bennett, Shade, Wright, Bishop, Pflegar, Webster, and Barry.

Members of the 1916 Conshohocken football team pose for a photograph. Conshohocken started the 1916 season by defeating its first five opponents, outscoring them 210-0. On November 4, the Carlisle Indians came to town. Following a near riot on the field, the game was declared a forfeit, and Conshohocken continued its three-year undefeated streak posting a 28-0-1 record. Members of the 1916 team include, from left to right, the following: (first row) Gravinese, Kennedy, Armitage, Hordtig, Kriebel, Potteiger, Hopkins, Moyer, Campbell, Fisher, Loughry, Briscko, and Gravinese; (second row) Hyde, Thomas, Bergy, Carter, Webster, unidentified, Jones, unidentified, Yeabsley, Fisher, Crawford, Pownall, Soap, Bergey, Mitchell, and Riggs.

On November 4, 1916, the Conshohocken professional football team played a game against the Carlisle Indians, shown above. The Indians were led by coach Morton Clevett, seen standing in the back row on the left. In the opening minutes of the second half, a near riot broke out when players got into a scuffle. Clevett pulled his team from the field and raced down Fayette Street toward the train station for a quick exit. Once the crowd heard the Indians were paid $300 for the game, the more than 4,000 angry fans chased the Indians down Fayette Street. Clevett and several players who did not make the train to Philadelphia were locked up in the Hector Street jail. Federal authorities became involved because the Indians were government property, and the local police had no jurisdiction over the team members or coaches. Members of the Carlisle team include, from left to right, (first row) Leroy, Herman, and Miles; (second row) Goes, Flinchum, Godfrey, May, Eshelman, Teeteske, and Ojibway; (third row) Clevett, Francis, White, Spears, Nori, Wills, and Smith.

The St. Matthew's High School football club, not sponsored by the school, played for a number of years as an independent team. Games were played on the bottom of John Elwood Lee's golf course between Ninth and Tenth Avenues on Wood Street. Members of the 1915 club include (first row) James Blake, Joseph Higgins, James McDade, Francis DeWan, and Thomas Keenan; (second row) John McNamara, Bill Collins, Jim McFadden, Jim Solger, Matt Getzfread, and Bill Carroll.

Members of the 1915 undefeated Conshohocken team include, from left to right, the following: (first row) mascots Gordon Atkins and Dewey Briscoe; (second row) Howard Armitage, Bill Hartig, Frank Kriebel (captain), Jack Shade, Llewellyn "Blubber" Jones, and Billy Williams; (third row) referee ? Hopkins, Terrence "Pick" Campbell, Percy Wright, Billy Pownall, Bert Yeabsley, Earl Potteiger, and Rube Kilpatrick; (fourth row) Olden Bishop, Sally Webster, Hoppy Pennington, Jim Schall, "Big Phil," Bob Crawford (manager), Harry Bergey, ? Carter, Seth Mitchell, Paul Pfleger, and assistant manager Ed Hyde.

FOOTBALL

The 1919 Conshohocken football team posted a 9-0 record. Years later, the Pro Football Hall of Fame declared the team champions of the Eastern Seaboard Professional Football League, and for many years, a photograph of Conshohocken's 1919 team was on display there. Members of the 1919 team include, from left to right, the following: (first row) Bechtel, Cable, Hartig, Bergey, Williams, and Jones; (second row) Yeabsley, Thomas, Wolavie, Eyrick, and Fisher; (third row) Crawford (manager), Rigg, Potteiger, Hallowell, Burkhart, Eble, Mitchel, Seaholtz, Campbell, and Hyde.

Members of the Polish American Club football team pose for a team photograph in the mid-1920s. Notice the high-top shoes and leather helmets; keep in mind that helmets were optional back then. The Polish American Club was one of many clubs in the 1920s to field football teams that played at the Conshohocken Community Field, where this photograph was taken.

Conshohocken's 1921 professional team posted an 11-1-1 record, scoring 175 points and allowing only 38. Conshohocken's big victory came over the Frankford Yellowjackets 14-7, but the team lost on Thanksgiving Day to the Philadelphia Quakers 12-0 in a driving rain. Members of the 1921 team include, from left to right, the following: (first row) Baker, Yeabsley, Mitchell, Rosetsky, Roundtree, Garrett, Shaffer, Fisher, Gotwals, and Isenburg; (second row) Ryan, Mackert, Bergy, Hart, Duff, Lukens, Burnheart, Archer, Doering, Riggs, and Potteiger.

The 1921–1922 Conshohocken Reliance football team won 18 games in two years, losing to Allentown 12-7 and to Shomoksin 12-6. Many of these players went on to play with the Conshohocken professional team in 1923. Chick Krieble captained this team, and other members of the team include Bill Douglass, Jim "Yippy" Fondots, Way, Gavin, Nevins, McCall, Davis, Johnson, Millhouse, Graul, Jones, Hanlon, Mason, Waktin, Quigg, Craig, Kriebel, Murphy, Dewees, and Hissner.

Joe Witt's Tigers, who played in the 1920s, are pictured from left to right: (first row) Felix "Flick" Hentz, Steve Tadawoski, Timmy Hayes, Ed McAvoy, John "Burke" Borkowski, Jimmy Bostok, and John "Skinny" Rozetski; (second row) Harry "Gump" Rowland, Ted "Dorman" Duraczynski, Ted Pope, William McAvoy, Andrew Pasquini, and Joe Smolinski; (third row) manager Joe Witt, John "Doc" Doughtery, Mike Rakowski, Stanley "Stosh" Shivik, Jimmy "Skates" Laskiewicz, Ed Krajewski, and coach Parry Murphy.

Football at Conshohocken High School was sanctioned in 1921, and all home games were played at the community field. In 1923, the team posted a 4-2-2 record, beating West Conshohocken 44-0. Posing here are, from left to right, (first row) Emmerson Webster, Gordon Atkins, Nicholas Talone, "Tinker" Rowan, and Charles Kendregan; (second row) Ray Stark, Winfield Crawford, James Pettine, Stanley Montgomery, Herbert Barron, William Neil, and George Bell; (third row) Francis Dennis, Harold Bishop, Wilfred Ruth, coach "Dutch" German, Ray Wilmer, Joseph Bates, and Roy Holden.

The 1924 Conshohocken High School football team posted a 5-3-2 season record, knocking off a very tough Haverford High School 26-9 and garnering a 14-0 win over Spring City. Quarterback Wood and running backs Kunkle, Wilmer, and Bates provided all the scoring for the Conshohocken High School team, and Holden, Dennis, and Prizer all had favorable write-ups in the local newspapers in 1924.

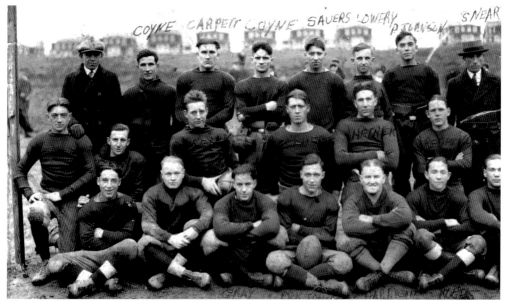

Sherwood Athletic Club football teams played in the borough throughout the 1920s and fielded some of the toughest teams in Montgomery County. All the players on this 1924 squad are not known, but standing in the back are, from left to right starting with second from left, J. Coyne, Carpett, Coyne, Sauers, Lowery, P. Johnson, and Snear. In the center row same order are V. Gray (second from left), Kelly, George Sauers, Hetrick, and Redmond. Seated in the front row are, from left to right, Johnson, unidentified, Gray, Pick Johnson, Harrison, Rogers, and unidentified.

The 1925 Sherwood Athletic Club football team includes, from left to right, the following: (first row) ? Beaver, Russell Gray, Buck Ruth, Tom Pick, ? Johnson, Elmer Harrison, Eggy Campbell, Anthony "Shorty" Roth, and Mutt Pope; (second row) Howard Gray, Carl Hertrick, Eddie Wernick, Benny Squers, Chippy Carpinet, and Jimmy Johnson; (third row) Elmer Lowry, Mickey Harrington, Ray Boyce, unidentified, Marty McCauley, Al Rosley, Jack Irwin, Jim Perseo, Jincus Coyne, Frank Rodenbaugh (manager) Ed Irwin, ? Renshaw, Joe "Blower" Kelly, and Johnny Boyce.

The St. Matthew's High School football team played six games in 1925, winning just two and losing the final game of the year to Conshohocken High School 40-6. Members of the team include, from left to right, the following: (first row) Francis Shinners, Joe Mullen, Leo Redmond, John Kilcoyne, Lawrence Hissner, and Joe Botto; (second row) Ed Rafferty, John McCruden, John Rafferty, Lou Devaney, John Fineran, and Al Quinn; (back row) Bill Wacker, coach Bill Carson, Fr. Thomas Peleshek, George Rafferty (manager), and Joe Carolin (assistant manager).

Johnny McBride, seen here in 1925, was Conshohocken's greatest football player to ever hail from this borough. McBride was an All-American at Syracuse University in 1924, before going on to play on the first New York Giants football team in 1925. McBride played halfback, quarterback, and punter and in 1925 ran out of the backfield with the great Jim Thorpe. He played 10 seasons in the NFL and was named MVP in 1927.

One of the many club football teams of the 1920s was the 1926 St. Mary's Connaughtown team that included those seen here. They are Julio Coccia, Carmen Zinni, Frank Rydal, Ricky Carlino, William Dorazio, Kiddi "Doc" Coccia, Frank Rodenbaugh, Joe Nardulli, John Russer, "Sixty" Monacella, Jim Kiser, Arthur Bruno, Al Dewees, Ernie Pettine, Bobby Kiser, Patsy Turk, John Muller, John Coshin, and Joe Kelly.

In 1927, St. Matthew's High School beat Conshohocken High School 7-0 when Lou Devaney scored the winning touchdown with just over two minutes remaining. Included here are, from left to right, the following: (first row) ? Kelly, Joseph Leary, Joe Mullen, Jim Fineran, Mark Quinn, Lou Devaney, Larry Hissner, Bob Hanna, Frank Burns, Ed Schrack, and Al Moore; (second row) George Rafferty (manager), Ed Dougherty, Joe Jones, coach Bill Carson, Bill O'Rourke, Roy Craft, Pud Weber, Ed Clark, John Devaney, Bud Keyser, and Fr. Thomas Peleshek.

Cap Smith's 1927 All Stars are pictured in December prior to a benefit game. The team earned a 12-0 victory over the Second Warders. Jimmy Brown scored both touchdowns. The All Stars include, from left to right, the following: (first row) Bud Ingram, Jack Irwin, Joe Nally, John Doughterty, Heads Nestor, Joe Murphy, Tom Watkins, and Legs Grauel; (second row) George Cross, Joe Douglass, Binty Paugh, Pud Russell, Bonus Thwaite, Elmer Millhouse, Jimmy Brown, Tom Douglass, Roy Douglass, Alf Dewees, Pat Donovan, Jack Frost, Joe Lafferty, Shorty York, and manager George Smith.

This photograph, taken at Hagar's Studio on Fayette Street, was used as a program cover for the Conshohocken Professionals football team in October 1928. The cover announced Conshohocken's Four Horsemen and chief of the Conshohocken Police Department, Daniel Donovan. The four horsemen are, from left to right, Walter Johnson, Charles Irwin, Edward Irwin, and Robert Hissner. The Pros (as they were known), while playing Chester in the opening game of the season, rolled to a 39-0 victory behind the fine coaching of Sam Knight.

The Desimone's Poolroom football team of 1928 includes, from left to right, (first row) Sol Desimone (manager), Morgan Mason, Bill "Sailor" Wertz, John Bonkowski, John "Bolwer" Kelly, Hugh "Huck" Gallagher, Sol "Bruno" Pastino, George Silk, Henry Leightham, and Bill Moriarity; (second row) Anthony "Rope" Ferst, unidentified, Bud Wannop, unidentified, Walt "Benny" Sauer, Joe Whip, Bennie "Burke" Borkowski, Ed Wernick, Costo Benidict, Bill O'Donnell, Charles Moriarity, Peter Koldys, Harold Halliday, Charles "Buck" Ramsey, Rod Engles, Joe Cavanaugh, and Walt (Wally) Drapikowski.

Members of the 1930 undefeated Conshohocken High School football team pose for a photograph following the final game of the season. Among those pictured are manager E. Longacre, R. Sponar, A. Bean, E. Dalby, J. Light, W. Yocum, B. Freas, W. Cubberly, J. Finklestein, head coach Maxwell R. Grimmett, manager O. Freas Jr., F. Gormley, E. Love, J. Koch, W. Becker, R. Farlie, R. Smith, V. Bonkoski, R. Tees, A. Riker, J. DelBuno, F. Lauletta, ? Ground, F. DePaulo, L. Limbert, J. Hipple, G. Pettine, M. Hipple, C. Earl, H. Rollins, and M. Bonkoski.

In the 1930s, professional football players did not make a lot of money; most players could pocket between $10 and $50 per game, depending on their skill. James Francis McMullen was a standout player and played for a number of teams in the 1930s. He lived on West Third Avenue before moving to West Conshohocken.

The Hollyhocks, who played in the 1920s, were made up of residents mostly from the lower end of West Fifth and Sixth Avenues. Mickey Harrington, standing in the back center, managed the team. George Sauers is in the middle row second from left; Sunny Bickings is next to Sauers in the middle row, third from left; and J. Coyne is next to Bickings. In the front row on the far right is Joe Carpineta, known as "Chippy," who later owned and operated Chippy's Grill, once located at West Sixth Avenue and Maple Street. (Courtesy of Patty Sauers Hunt.)

Members of the 1931 Conshohocken Catholic Club line up for a photograph taken in the Meadow, once located on Washington and Cherry Streets. Members are, from left to right, (first row) Joe Baranoski, Pat Bolton, Conrad Swalla, Jesse Zadroga, Jo-Jo Podbielski, Whitey Baldyga, and Eddie Polkowski; (second row) Shorty Bruno, Tony Shivick, Joe Wyrwas, Jimmy Grauel, and Binkie Farley.

The Conshohocken Pros of 1936 are seen during the opening kickoff at the Conshohocken Community Center field. Conshohocken beat Riverside, New Jersey, 20-0 and posted a 7-2-4 record in 1936 for a first-place finish in the league but lost the championship game to Passayunk 3-2. In the Riverside game, coach Hannigan scored two touchdowns and Zadroga scored a touchdown and kicked the extra points as well. The 1936 team was led by O'Donnell, Lawler, Hobson, Zadroga, Miller, and Worrall.

In 1938, the Conshohocken professional football team won a championship in the Eastern Pennsylvania Football Conference. It turned in an 11-3 record, losing to rival Norristown LAM but beating them in the championship game 14-0. Conshohocken players warming up at Philadelphia's Shibe Park before the championship game, seen here, include Preston "Peppy" Campbell (standing on the left), Ira "Whitey" Mellor (in the backfield), Al Oliver (standing on the left), Mac Simon (the left tackle), and Knute Lawler (standing at the left end position).

The Conshohocken Pros of the 1940s fielded some pretty good teams led by Whitey Mellor, Peppy Campbell, Jesse Zadroga, Harvey Borzellecca, and Dan O'Donnell. The 1940s teams were coached by Harry Fox. The Conshohocken Community Field had covered grandstands in the 1930s and 1940s, but renovations in 1947, paid for by Albert A. Garthwaite and the Lee Tire and Rubber Company, led to new grandstands that were no longer covered.

Members of the Cosmian Catholic Club lined up for a team photograph in the late 1940s. The sport of football had advanced a long way from the 1920s: the scoring was different, padding for protection was truly advanced, and players made the game much faster, forcing most running backs to wear leather helmets. The Cosmian Catholic Club played for several years in different leagues and was one of dozens of football teams playing in Conshohocken at the time.

For nearly two decades, "Big Dan" O'Donnell was one of the best athletes of his era. A St. Matthew's High School product, O'Donnell lettered and starred in all the schools sports and really excelled in basketball. But after high school, O'Donnell played on a number of baseball, football, and basketball teams, including a five-year stint with the Conshohocken professional football team.

George Lucey (No. 23), in the third row, third from left, poses with his Marine Corps all-star football team in China in 1948. Lucey, a 1946 graduate of St. Matthew's High School, was a first-string end on the team that finished in second place in the Marine Corps League in China. Lucey was a first-string football player for the Marine Corps and named to the Marine Corps all-star team. (Courtesy of George Lucey.)

While Conshohocken High School did not have a successful season in 1942, it played all the top area schools, including Norristown, Phoenixville, and Pottstown. Pictured are, from left to right, (first row) Novi, Pasquini, Carosello, Ristine, Andraka, Nixon, Opelski, DiJosia, and DeCamillo; (second row) Pellegrino, Graham, Sirchio, Pinelli, Irwin, Woyden, Mundy, Buds, Andraka, Williamson, and Travagline; (third row) DeWalt, Link, Kasopsky, Murray, Stubinski, Zajac, Peszak, and O'Donnell.

In 1947, Conshohocken High School and St. Matthew's High School football teams met on the Bridgeport field for their annual Thanksgiving Day game, which ended in a scoreless tie. Here a coin toss determines which school will hold the Lions Club trophy for the following year. On the left is Joe Golas, captain of the Conshohocken team, shaking hands with Michael Moore, captain of St. Matthew's High School squad.

FOOTBALL

Senior members of the St. Matthew's High School squad are lined up for this photograph in 1954 at Sutcliffe Park. They are, from left to right, (first row) Ted Leszczynski, Jim Haines, Tom Smith, Curt Hissiner, and Dave Carroll; (second row) Jake Murphy, John Pilcicki, Sterling Devlin, Dan Wilson, and Jim O'Connor. Donald Brady, the team's other senior, is not in the picture.

Conshohocken Elementary School fifth graders pose after a championship season in November 1955. Shown are, from left to right, (first row) Henry Griffith, Don Bosco, Gerald Moore, Lenny Weidman, George Doughtery, Joseph Nolan, and David Minnick; (second row) Ralph Bolger, Harold Jones, Edward Manning, Michael Ethridge, Jim Battle, and Charles Haines.

Conshohocken High School enjoyed its most successful years in the 1950s, posting 52 victories on the gridiron. In 1955, Jerry "Reds" Pettine is carrying the ball at the Conshohocken Community Field during a 19-0 victory over rival Plymouth Whitemarsh High School. While the 1955 Conshohocken squad posted a 6-4 season record, head coach Ray Weaver enjoyed the 26-0 Thanksgiving Day victory over St. Matthew's High School.

The Conshohocken midget football program was founded in 1961 with four teams. The four teams were named the Bobcats, Blue Devils, Wild Cats, and Tigers. The midgets did not take on the Golden Bears logo until after Conshohocken High School closed in 1966. Members of several teams and coaches pose in this 1967 photograph taken at the Conshohocken A Field.

FOOTBALL

Throughout the 1960s and 1970s, the West Conshohocken Raiders midget football team was an excellent program for children in the borough. In the mid-1970s, West Conshohocken mayor George Barr takes time out to chat with a number of players from the Raiders organization. (Courtesy of the Barr family.)

In the fall of 1971, members of the Conshohocken Golden Bears cheerleading squads line up for a group photograph taken at the Conshohocken B Field, where the football teams and cheerleaders practiced. In 1971, the Golden Bears organization was celebrating 10 years, having been chartered in 1961.

CONSHOHOCKEN AND WEST CONSHOHOCKEN SPORTS

The Conshohocken Steelers started out in the mid-1960s as a semiprofessional football team called the Irontown Athletic Association. Later named the Steelers, the team played for more than a decade in the Seaboard League. The 1972 Steelers seen in the photograph above were coached by John Vernachio. By the late 1970s, the team disbanded, only to reemerge in the late 1980s. By the early 1990s, the Steelers were winning championships on a regular basis. The 1992 team shown below includes Ed and Steve Borkowski, Barry Doganieri, John Kelly, John Leszcynski, Al Torcini, and Keith Galie, just to name a few.

Longtime Archbishop Kennedy High School football coach Chris Bockrath, above center, is seen here coaching for Kennedy Kenrick High School in 1994 and was one of the most beloved coaches in recent history. Bockrath, seen with coach Paul Balzano on the right and Dominick D'Addona on the left in the photograph above, coached for Archbishop Kennedy High School for 19 years. Following a school merger, Bockrath coached for three more years at the high school before moving on to Delaware Valley College. Bockrath posted eight Bicentennial League titles and three more cochampionship titles while coaching Kennedy. In the photograph below, Bockrath is seen celebrating his 100th victory as a high school head coach in 1991.

Enjoying life as a teenager in 1947 at a St. Matthew's High School football game at the Conshohocken A Field are, from left to right, (first row) Marie Zadroga and Dolores Spring; (second row) Florence Cherry and Terry Podbilski. St. Matthew's High School was playing Panther Valley High School, a game that St. Matthew's lost 18-6, but the team managed a 4-4-1 record in 1947. (Courtesy of Florence Cherry Barolt.)

St. Matthew's High School cheerleaders pose for a photograph during halftime of a football game in the fall of 1947. St. Matthew's students attended the Hector Street school before moving to 1300 Fayette Street in 1956. Posing are, from left to right, (first row) Ann Marie Deliah, Helen Mitch, and Pat Lacey; (second row) Margie Coonok, Pat Rath, and Florence Cherry. (Courtesy of Florence Cherry Barolt.)

2

BASEBALL

Roy "Whitey" Ellam is shown perhaps from his playing days in Ambler in 1907 or in 1908 when he played professional baseball in Connellsville. Ellam, who went on to play with the Cincinnati Reds and the Pittsburgh team, was born and raised in West Conshohocken. As a manager, nicknamed the "Miracle Man," he led a number of southern teams to championships. In 1918, while playing with Pittsburgh, Ellam played in the longest scoreless game in the history of professional baseball. (Courtesy of the Ellam family.)

Conshohocken's first recorded baseball games and local teams date as far back as the mid-1880s. The game quickly became popular, and by 1895, when this team photograph was taken, dozens of teams for all ages formed in Conshohocken. Besides the many industrial teams formed before 1900, other teams took the field like the Young Men's Athletic Association (YMAA), the Tammany Tigers, the Park Club, the Rockets, and the Third Avenue Boys. There was a team called the Crushers, and Connaughtown fielded both junior and senior teams. A few of the members of this team are identified, including, from left to right, (first row) Francis Cresson and Art Clark; (second row) Fred Clark, Sam Wright, Eugene Beaver, and unidentified; (third row unidentified, ? O'Neill, Matt Tracy, ? Schwartz, Harry Moats, and ? O'Neill.

The Pastime Club of West Conshohocken, founded in 1903, sponsored various teams for more than 20 years, including championship baseball teams and pool teams. In 1913, the cribbage team was Montgomery County champion. This photograph from the summer of 1911 shows one of the teams that played its games at Mud Hollow Field. Not all the players are identified, but in the first row are, from left to right, Ed Flanagan, Bob McDowell, Steve Ferrier, and Tom Flanagan. In the second row are, from left to right, Pup McLaughlin, ? Pope, Joe Garnet, Cliff Williams, and Jack Welsh. In the third row are, in no particular order, Ed Smith, ? Pope, Jack Smith, and ? Gehris.

More than a half-dozen semiprofessional baseball teams from Conshohocken and West Conshohocken played the game in the Meadow in 1912 when this picture was taken of the Conshohocken Athletic Club team. William Parry Murphy and Walt Mason, both seen in the back row, were very good baseball players back in the day and helped the athletic club to a championship season in 1912.

Members of the John Wood baseball team pose for this photograph in 1921. In the early days of the sport, industrial league members of the team had to be employed by the firm that they represented in the field of sports. Seen here are, from left to right, (first row) B. Kennedy, ? Jeleski, B. Williams, J. Wheeler, and L. Widner; (second row) C. Rein, H. Hamill, R. Boyce, A. Maryland, E. Munro, C. Moser, and R. Blake.

In 1922, when this picture was taken of the John Wood baseball team, the company had won the championship, taking two of three from Lee Tire for the trophy. Pictured are, from left to right, (first row) William Kennedy, William Maggio, Frank Zeleski, Howard Oliver, George Carney, and William Willias; (second row) James McTamney, Howard Longacre, Francis McCall, Walter Lacey (manager), Michael Burns (assistant manager), Harvey Longacre, Elmer Monroe, and Clyde Moser.

BASEBALL

In 1927, members of the West Conshohocken High School baseball team posed for this team photograph. Included in the photograph are, from left to right, (first row) Alfred Rissell, Robert Reid, Howard Ferrier, Joseph Ingram, Paul Adams, and Gilbert Sowers; (second row) William H. Brown (principal and coach), Lester Cox, Earnest Panldids, Howard Custer, Paul Harper, John Blair, and Norman Rush.

The 1929 Conshohocken High School baseball team displays its two championship trophies having won the Montgomery County section of the Class C Suburban League on the arm of Perk Smith in a victory over Jenkintown. The team also won the lower section of Montgomery County, beating Bridgeport 10-9 in a close game. Coach Maxwell R. Grimmett led the Conshy nine to their second straight championship behind the fine play of Smith, Bonkoski, Webster, Godshalk, and Fairlie.

Baseball was one of the earliest sports played in the borough of Conshohocken; traced back to the early 1880s, a team called the Nerve of Conshohocken played other local teams, on a field called the Meadow, down by the river. Many teams followed over the next century, including teams from the Spring Mill section of Conshohocken. The early Spring Mill teams played many of their games at the Spring Mill Country Club. Opposing teams would travel by train on Saturday and Sunday afternoons where large crowds would gather to cheer on the locals. In later years, boys representing the Spring Mill Fire Company would field teams playing many other local teams in the Montgomery County area. The photograph above of the Spring Mill team was taken in the early 1930s, while the photograph below was taken in the early 1960s.

Members of the St. Mark's Lutheran Church baseball team pose after winning the Church League championship in the summer of 1932. Seated in front of the trophy is batboy Bill Gilinger Jr. Also seated are, from left to right, (first row) Bill Sweimler Sr., Park Fraelic (later lost in action during World War II), Shay Cummins, and John Sparrow (manager); (second row) Fred Fairlie Jr., Jack Palmer, Chief Murray Jr., and Harold Krieble Sr.; (third row) Bill Sweimler Jr. and Al Rissel. Standing on the left is Chester Freas, and on the right is Rev. Pat McCarney.

The St. Mary's Young Men's Catholic Club (YMCC) baseball team played in several leagues throughout the 1930s and 1940s, including the Norristown Baseball League and the Polish Suburban Catholic League. Among those pictured are J. Misko, B. Kelly, John Sedur, Joe Dolewa, T. Gatta, Shorty Olkewicz, J. Conway, Buff Nattles, ? Cerankowski (manager), Tom Smith, Frank Zadroga, Harry Coven, Mike Skelly, and Adam Hylinski.

Gerald Nugent (left), president and owner of the Philadelphia Phillies, talks with Connie Mack, owner of the Philadelphia A's. Nugent signed a lease with Mack in 1938 because his Phillies were no longer playing their games on the Baker Bowl Field but were moving five blocks north on Lehigh Avenue to Shibe Park. Nugent and his wife, Mae, owned the Philadelphia Phillies from 1933 to 1942, and they lived in Conshohocken on Fayette Street during their ownership. (Courtesy of Temple University Urban Archives.)

In 1940, America was still in peacetime, industry in Conshohocken was at an all-time high, jobs were plenty, and families thrived in the borough. Industrial baseball teams in town were plentiful with companies like Walker Brothers, Hale Pumps, Alan Wood Steel, and John Wood manufacturing companies participating in the Industrial League loop. Members of the 1940 Lee Tire and Rubber Company baseball team pose for a team photograph.

Members of the 1942 Conshohocken High School baseball team pose for a team picture following the 1942 season. The Bears came in second place of the Suburban League Section Six that year with a 5-4 record. Notable games came against Bridgeport, when the Bears beat the Dragons twice, including a 5-3 victory where Joe Stubinski struck out 17 batters. Stubinski, an All-Suburban basketball standout, also pitched a no-hitter the following week against West Conshohocken High School.

The Conshohocken Police Athletic League (PAL) formed a baseball league in the early 1950s for children. Some of the players, managers, and officers of the 1953 league included those seen above. They are, from left to right, (first row) Sgt. Charles Marwood (PAL president), Larry Hissner, "Slip" Mahoney, Leslie Williamson, Tommy Priest, and Bill Bozarth (PAL vice president); (second row) Charles Butera (PAL treasurer), Joe Bry, Jack Whalen, Bob Leroy, patrolman Matthew Doughtery, and Robert Carroll (PAL secretary); (third row) John Sparrow (manager), Enoch Zapien, Richard Pasquarello, Joe Nosek, John Hildebrand, and Robert Slater (manager).

In the late 1950s and early 1960s, much of Sutcliffe Park was still undeveloped. The 37-acre tract on the west side of the borough was donated in 1930 by Frank Sutcliffe in honor of his wife, Mary Jane. The park now has five baseball fields, basketball courts, a playground, and a walking track.

Conshohocken Little League was established in 1955, and by 1959, the Fellowship House established a minor league because the Little League had only four teams with room for 48 boys to play (no girls were allowed in Little League in the 1950s). When the Fellowship House put out the call for baseball players, more than 250 boys signed up to play at the Conshohocken A Field. In this photograph from 1960, some of the young men learn the finer points of the game.

BASEBALL

In 1969, this photograph was taken at the annual Conshohocken Babe Ruth Baseball League awards banquet. Shown in the first row are the manager and coach from the championship team that year, Pat Campellone (left) and Ken White, respectively. Standing in the back are, from left to right, Herb O'Byrne, outstanding 13-year-old player award; Larry Bowe, sportsmanship winner; Steve Kozeniewski, most improved; Denny Gordon, MVP; and Emil Civerilli, league president.

Bill McAvoy, standing in the back row on the left, was a coach and manager for many years with St. Matthew's Catholic Youth Organization (CYO). McAvoy poses with his coaches and players from the 1993 girls' softball team. The Conshohocken CYO program at one time included St. Mary's, St. Matthew's, and SS. Cosmas and Damian churches.

Throughout the 1980s and 1990s, Archbishop Kennedy High School fielded some very talented sports teams. Five members of the 1989 softball team pose for this photograph, and while it is not clear who told the joke, it must have been a real knee-slapper according to the reaction of the players. Posing are, from left to right, Diane Mann, Megan Gebhardt, Karen Lawrence, Kristine Lesher, and Christine Fleming.

BASEBALL

The Plymouth Whitemarsh High School baseball team will forever be remembered in the Conshohocken area for a game it played on June 16, 1994. The team traveled to Williamsport for a showdown with the North Allegheny Tigers in a one-game playoff for the Pennsylvania Interscholastic Athletic Association (PIAA) Class AAA state championship. In the bottom of the seventh and final inning with the score tied at 4-4, Eric Fisher reached out on a 1-2 pitch and delivered a base hit to right field scoring Matt Alteri from second base for the winning run. Although the throw beat Alteri to the plate, his head-first slide allowed him to avoid the tag, and in a dramatic moment, the Plymouth Whitemarsh team had won a state championship. Below, some of the fans react to the victory.

Harry Fox, seen in his United States Marines baseball uniform in 1945, became a beloved manager and coach at Conshohocken High School and later at Upper Merion High School, where he served as a coach and athletic director for many years. Fox was an assistant coach at Conshohocken High School from 1937 to 1939, was head coach from 1940 to 1941, then departed for the war where he played with the 4th Naval District Marines in 1945. After the war, he returned to manage from 1946 to 1958. Fox also coached football and the Conshohocken professional teams in the 1940s.

3

LITTLE LEAGUE BASEBALL

In 1958, more than 300 boys attended tryouts at Sutcliffe Park for less than 20 openings in Conshohocken Little League. In 1959, the league expanded to six teams and games were moved to Sutcliffe Park. All games were previously played at Rossi Memorial Field behind the Conshohocken Bocce Club (CBC) on Third Avenue. Ange D'Amico, manager of the Orioles, is on hand to help the youngsters try out, including Billy Johnson, batting, and Jerry Gray, catching.

Conshohocken Little League, formed in 1955, played its games at the CBC on West Third Avenue until 1959, when the league moved to Sutcliffe Park. The 1955 Blue Jays, sponsored by the John Wood Company, are, from left to right, (first row) Eugene Cichetti, Bob Graham, Frank Graham, Jim DiCiurcio, and Tyrone Smith; (second row) Lou Capelli (manager), Tom Moore, Joe Slovak Jr., Calvin Flowers, John Vischi, Joe Mariani, and Joe Slovak; (third row) John Berheiter, Ted Pierce, Ken Hissner, coach Larry Hissner (standing behind), Tony Moore, and Dave Havener.

Members of the 1958 Conshohocken Little League Cardinals line up at the start of the league's third season at Rossi Memorial Field. The team coaches are Reds Harrison (left) and Joe McFadden, and players, in no special order, include Phil Gravinese, Phil Januzelli, Dave Reed, Pete DiDonato, Henry Griffith, Sam Dituro, Bob Pasquarello, Jim LePera, Jim DiSante, Charlie Gambone, Bob Moore, Mike Ethridge, Roger Allen, Joe McFadden and Fran Januzelli.

LITTLE LEAGUE BASEBALL

In 1957, Conshohocken Little League had great support from the community, which supported four major-league teams. Members of the Orioles team include coach Adam Pagliaro, standing in the back on the left, and head coach Ange D'Amico, standing on the right; the players included are, in no special order, Jim Murphy, Joe Tadeo, Jack Mangum, Joe Cross, Joe Leary, Bill Gordon, George DiCiurcio, Dave Minnick, Jim Pishock, Jim Harener, Les Rissell, Joe Logan, Bill Maher, Bill Collins, and Tony Giradi.

In 1958, the Conshohocken Little League Robins team had a good year led by manager Ray Gravinese. The players included Joe Iacovotti, George Pettine, John Casinelli, Stan Czermanski, Stan Rakowski, Pete DePallo, Russ Bogle, Anthony Gambale, Bob Kerns, John Novak, Abe Kitt, Tom White, Paul Dunn, Dennis Doughtery, and Richard Leddy.

In 1959, Conshohocken Little League's board of directors built a new ball field at Sutcliffe Park. The project was headed by Ray and Phil Gravinese, and the outfield fence was built at Franny Carr's garage, at Tenth Avenue and Forrest Street. The fence was installed at Rossi Memorial Field in 1956 and relocated to Sutcliffe Park in 1959. Installing the fence in the photograph above are, from left to right, Ange D'Amico, ? Romano, Herman Tatito, and Phil Gravinese. Finishing the outfield fence in the photograph below are, from left to right, Little Leaguers Norman Santangelo and Terrance Toole and Romano.

Opening day in 1959 was a major event in Conshohocken Little League history. It was the opening of another season and dedication of a new Little League field at Sutcliffe Park. League officials taking part in the opening day ceremonies in 1959 include, from left to right, (first row) Jimmy Verrone and Phil Gravinese; (second row) Ange D'Amico, Bob Wesley, John Casinelli, Joe Dennis, and Ray Gravinese.

Handing out trophies at the 1960 Conshohocken Little League banquet are coaches and league officials. In the back row are, from left to right, Alfred "Cap" Januzelli, Franny Traviline, Frank Palermo Jr., and Knute Silverstrini. Happy trophy recipients being honored for their first-place finish in the front include Phil Januzelli, holding the trophy, and Bob Wesley.

Conshohocken Little Leaguers gathered in 1961 to check out a list of golfers who were participating in a benefit tournament at the Oak Terrace Country Club with proceeds going to Conshohocken Little League. From left to right at the Little League field are John Lewkowicz, Chris Bockrath, John Casinelli (president of the league), Tom DiCiurcio, Phil Gravinese (golf committee chairman), Bobby Ramey, and Frank Palermo Jr. (also of the golf committee).

Members of the 1962 Conshohocken Little League Orioles pose for a team photograph. Ange D'Amico, standing in the back row on the left, was the manager, and Frank Burton, on the right, was the coach. Team members include John Waszena, Bernard Murray, William Schank, Walter Wienczek, Michael Hayes, Ken Bate, David Ottey, Anthony Baranowski, Bruce Bonkoski, Richard Mellor, Jay Kunaszuk, Ed Burton, George Falconero, Paul Zadroga, and Thomas Kielinski.

Award recipients are all smiles at the 1962 Conshohocken Little League banquet. On the left, Charles Jeffries displays his sportsmanship award. John Lewkowicz holds the team's first-place trophy, and on the far right, Tom Grayauski holds the MVP award. Standing in the back are, from left to right, James Verrone and Richard Kosek, manager and coach of the first-place team; Dick Porter, former major-league outfielder and guest speaker; and Frank Palermo Jr., league treasurer.

Members of the 1963 Orioles baseball team in the Conshohocken Little League pose for a picture on opening day of the season. Standing from left to right are Jay Kunaszuk, Bernie Murray, Jimmy Zaleski, Jimmy Young, and Joe Dawidzick.

In 1965, Frank Herron was president of the Conshohocken Little League, which consisted of six teams with 15 players on each team. The Hawks team in 1965 included Mike DePallo, Jerome Galie, Larry Bowe, Larry Cermanski, Johnny Pasquarello, Paul Kurkowski, Frank Herron, Wallace Taraborrelli, Dave Donovan, Mike Hatfield, Walt Napierkowski, Charles Donahue, Tom Plower, Richard Tancini, and Dennis Gordon. Gasper Scardino was the team manager, and Norman Santangelo was the coach.

John Bosak, standing in the back, was the manager for the 1965 Blue Jays. Team members include, in no special order, Russ Emele, Gary Shore, Gerry Weber, Joey Galette, Mike Borzelleca, Mike Cianci, John Larcinese, Frank Vermuth, Don Warner, John Plower, Paul Cunningham, Bill Kelly, John Heleniak, Steve Barkfski, and Billy Galette.

The 1965 Conshohocken Little League all-star team won a district title by beating West Norriton 12-1, their first district title since 1958. Members of the all-star team include, from left to right, (first row) Paul Kurkowski, Mike Piotrowski, Bucky Priest, Tom DiAnnunzio, and John Plower; (second row) Larry Tadeo, Tommy Plower, John Westerfer, Robin Woznicki, and Walt Naplerkowski; (third row) coach Frank Toby, Billy Galetti, Frank Herron, and manager Phil Gravinese.

Members of the 1967 Conshohocken Little League Orioles team pose on opening day at Sutcliffe Park. Manager Ange D'Amico, standing in the back on the left, coached or managed for 35 years in the league. His coach, on the right, was Joe Dennis. Members of the Orioles include, in no special order, Michael Barkofski, Frank Burton, Tom Connelly, Nick D'Annunzio, Matt Kelly, Frank Landi, Tony Maresca, Joe Morgan, David Murray, Jan Narciso, Bob O'Donnell, Tom O'Donnell, Matt Ryan, Paul Sarvey, and Bob Teaford.

The 1969 Eagles baseball team was sponsored by Marchak Lumber Company, then located on West Hector Street. George Warriner managed the Eagles, and Nick Cione was the coach. Members of the Eagles included Steve Waszena, Joe McCann, James Moyer, Robert Wells, Fred Kelly, Kenneth Hobbs, James Mullen, Robert Moyer, James D'Annunzio, Paul Stanish, Francis Minnick, Charles Lunney, Eric DiPasquale, James Muscon, and Dave Warriner.

The Philadelphia National Bank sponsored the Robins Little League team in 1969. The bank was the longest continuous sponsor in Conshohocken Little League history, sponsoring for more than 30 years. Norman Santangelo managed the 1969 Robins and team players are, in no special order, Dennis Donovan, Bill Connelly, Robert Richards, Joe Maresca, Richard Bolger, Jim McEvoy, Joe Kelly, Pat Getzfread, Tom Santoni, Ted Zoltowski, Dave Kurkowski, Mike Getzfread, John Weill, Jim DelBuno, and John Kelly.

Conshohocken Little League all-star teams have had some great success in District 22 over the years, and in 1975, John Maiden led the all-star team that includes, in no special order, John Pehine, David Baglivo, Jeff Schwartz, David Pehine, Chris Miszaros, Kevin Maiden, Gary Smith, Joe Benedict, Kevin Borusiewicz, Brian Wisniewski, Matt Brown, Danny Grayauski, and Jay Dolewa.

By 1984, Conshohocken Little League had grown to include the minor league and T-ball league, allowing players ages 6 to 12 and both boys and girls to play. Members of the Hawks in 1984 are, from left to right, Josh Dugas, Brian Coll, Dennis Daley, and Chris Griffin.

Opening day of the Conshohocken Little League season is always a big deal, and youngsters are eager and ready to play ball. In 1987, the manager of the Dodgers, Bob Frost, gives some opening day advice on pitching to these three young ballplayers, who are, from left to right, Sean Van Buskirk, Robert Frost, and Timmy Gunning.

On opening day in 1990, Ange D'Amico was honored by the league as he prepared to start his 36th season as a manager, coach, and board of directors member. D'Amico started with the league in 1955. Posing with D'Amico are, from left to right, Ricky Mellor, Robert Reed, Tommy Bruno, and Michael Maxwell.

SOAP BOX DERBY

The soap box derby in Conshohocken started in 1938 when 75 boys competed on Spring Mill Avenue in two brackets. Walt Cherry edged out Matthew O'Connor to win a new bicycle. More than 5,000 spectators lined Spring Mill Avenue. Cherry is seen sitting in his winning car in 1938. There was a $10 spending limit to build a car, and most drivers came in well under the limit. Cherry also won the 1939 event, also held on Spring Mill Avenue. (Courtesy of Florence Cherry Barolt.)

Before the Conshohocken Soap Box Derby race was sanctioned in 1952, a pushmobile race was held in 1951 on Fayette Street. Dave McQuirns is pictured here in his old No. 7 car. The race was from Eighth Avenue down to Sixth Avenue. McQuirns was the victor, beating out 10 other racers to win a bicycle valued at $52. Other racers competing in 1951 included Warren Moyer, Walter Swing, Larry Palacio, John Freeland, James Neve, David Frost, Tony Moore, Jerry Freas, Lowell Sibole, and Charles Frost.

These high ramps were used throughout the 1950s and early 1960s before being replaced with high metal ramps; by the early 1990s, a much lower ramp was put in use and is still used to this day. This photograph, taken in the mid-1950s, shows two drivers at the starting gate. The car on the right was sponsored by Clem's Meat Market.

In the early years of soap box derby racing in Conshohocken, parades and events were always a major part of the Fourth of July celebration. In 1953, Dolores Phipps was the winner of the title Miss Conshohocken Jaycee for 1953. Phipps was featured in both the Fourth of July firemen's parade and the annual soap box derby parade.

In 1953, more than 50 soap box derby racers are seen parading out of East Hector Street onto Fayette Street, wearing their official helmets and T-shirts. The derby contestants were usually led in the parade by the Joseph Wagner Post, fire trucks, and "Chuck Wagon Pete," a Conshohocken resident who appeared on many children's television shows throughout the 1950s and 1960s. As the drivers parade out onto Fayette Street, they pass the Banker's Tavern, Western Union, and McGoaigal's Drug Store.

Three of the official soap box derby cars that would compete in the July 4, 1953, race are on display at the Washington Fire Company. Seated in the car on the left is Jesse Stemple, in a car that was driven by Allen Phipps of West Conshohocken. In the middle is Robert Garnett of Sixth Avenue, and on the right is Danny Allerton of West Hector Street.

In 1953, three wooden ramps were used to race in three lanes down Fayette Street. Some 50 racers competed in 1953 for a single championship; there were no brackets. The following year the race used two ramps. Throughout the 1950s and 1960s, the event across the country was called "the Greatest Amateur Racing Event in the World for Boys." Females were not permitted to race in the All-American race event until a court handed down an order allowing girls to participate in the mid-1970s.

Lowell Sibole, sitting in his "Blue Clipper" soap box derby car in the photograph above after winning the 1953 race, accepts congratulations from the 1952 champion, John Kirkner. More than 8,000 spectators witnessed the 1953 annual soap box derby race. In the photograph below, in 1992, Sibole, with help from his daughter Kate, broke out some of the old memories from the 1953 derby and trip to the All-American race in Akron. Included are the Conshohocken banner that was flown on a street pole in Akron, the helmet that was worn for the All-American race, and Sibole's sideboard of the original car; notice Conshohocken spelled wrong.

In 1953, 15 of the 34 racers in the soap box derby race gather for a photograph in front of E. F. Moore Chevrolet, located at Twelfth and Fayette Streets. From left to right are (first row) Jimmy Burnett, Jack Schultz (seated in racer), Jack Joiner, and Dick Pettit; (second row) Jack Wright, Robert Wood, Nordie Hauk, and Jimmie Hilbert; (third row) Earl Watkins, Francis Collins, Francis Opelski, Tommy Sukalski, Lloyd Laskey, Tony Spineo, and Harry Milakeve. Lucky was the unofficial racing mascot.

Members of the Schwartz family gather before leaving for the All-American race. Paul S., seated in the center, won the 1964 Conshohocken derby when he beat James Koniewicz by three feet in a runoff heat after the two finished in a dead heat. He won a $500 savings bond and an all-expenses-paid trip to Akron, where he competed with more than 250 other racers. Seated are, from left to right, his father, Paul, Paul S., and his sister Lugene. Standing in the back are Paul S.'s mother, Catherine, on the left and his sister Paula. (Courtesy of Paula Schwartz Reed.)

Wearing the helmet in the photograph at right, 13-year-old Bob Cahill treats his cousin Mike Smith to a short ride in the parking lot of the Gulf gas station located at Fifth Avenue and Fayette Street. Cahill lost his first heat during the Conshohocken Soap Box Derby race in 1957. Cahill bounced back a year later to win a heat and was presented with a flashlight donated by Kehoe Hardware and an ice-cream maker. In the image below, Bob Cahill Sr. loads his son Bob onto the starting ramp for the 1991 soap box derby race. The race has been held on Fayette Street since 1951.

Conshohocken Soap Box Derby 1959 champion Tommy Carroll, second from right, accepts the 1959 Chevrolet N. E. Cole Award. Carroll beat out 48 other contestants for the honor of competing in Akron at the All-American race. Posing in the winners' circle on Fayette Street in 1959 are, from left to right, Bill Moore, an unidentified Chevrolet representative, Joe Bowe, Ed Moore, and Carroll. Looking on is the 1958 champion, John Lebold. In the photograph below, Carroll shows his racer off from two years earlier as he sits in his car at the top of the ramp waiting for the start of the race.

Throughout the 1950s and 1960s, soap box derby drivers met at the Washington Fire Company before the race and paraded up Fayette Street to Seventh Avenue, where Conshohocken High School was once located. For a number of years, television Channel 3's "Pistol Pete" Boyle led the parade to the high school where flag-raising ceremonies started the Fourth of July celebration. The Joseph Wagner Post leads the parade in this 1965 photograph, and the post members and drivers line up on West Hector Street to start their march.

Throughout the 1980s and early 1990s, the Conshohocken Ambucs ran the largest soap box derby special division race in the country. Peter Moore, standing on the side of the car helping the drivers onto the ramp, was president of the Conshohocken Ambucs when this photograph was taken. Codriver Charles O'Byrne is sitting on the left side of the car while driver Chris Moore is on the right.

It was a close race in 1986 when Jackie Coll, racing in the car sponsored by Joseph Rose Painting, raced against Chris Ciavarelli, whose car was sponsored by Ciavarelli's Funeral Home. About 40 racers competed for the championship in 1986, and when it was over, Leah Racich won the junior division, and Allisa DiCicco won the senior division. It was the second time in Conshohocken derby history that two females swept the derby.

Over the more than 60 years of soap box derby racing in Conshohocken, thousands of young boys and girls have participated in the All-American race event. Philip Dean in the front and Bob Pfanders in the back wait their turn in 1986.

Perhaps this photograph shows how far soap box derby has come over the years with the lay-back-style senior division cars looking more like a bullet than a car. In 1990, car handler Bob Frost helps his daughter Jessica with her helmet as she lays back in the car ready to race. Jessica was a former champion from 1988 and won third-place honors in 1990.

In recent years, Conshohocken Soap Box Derby racers have experienced a lot of success at the national level of racing, as Kristen Donovan did in 1993. Donovan finished fourth overall in the All-American race event held in Akron. She raced in the kit car division and came in ahead of about 75 other contestants in her division. Donovan is seen here as she arrives back in Conshohocken to a hero's welcome.

Three soap box derby veterans look over what they had hoped would be the winning car in 1996. From left to right are Tom Carroll, the 1959 Conshohocken derby champion, and his two brothers, Dave and Bob. The trio, with years of building and racing experience, all attended the final inspection to give Tom's son Tommy their stamp of approval before the car was impounded for race day. The young Carroll lost to Kelly Cline in the masters division.

In 1953, soap box derby racers line up on Fayette Street before the start of the second annual race in Conshohocken. Lowell Sibole, seen in the front on the far right, was the eventual winner. In 1953, a $25 spending limit on the car was part of the rule book. Sibole's father was working in the Spring Mill section of town and came across a couple old World War II airplane wings in a customer's yard. Those wings made perfect sides for a soap box derby car.

SOAP BOX DERBY

5

EVERY OTHER SPORT

Joey Hatfield was one of three Conshohocken boxers who were feared in the boxing circles throughout the tristate area of Pennsylvania, Delaware, and New Jersey. The trio also included Johnny Craven and Midget Fox. Together they fought more than 750 professional fights and a combined 150 amateur fights. In the 1920s, fights at the Conshohocken Community Field (also called the Conshohocken A Field), located at Eleventh Avenue and Harry Street, could draw up to 1,000 spectators to watch a triple-header fight on a Friday or Saturday night.

JOE HATFIELD

In August 1958, the Washington Fire Company sponsored an outdoor wrestling match at the Conshohocken A Field to benefit the fire company's need for a new 1,000-gallon-a-minute pumper. It had been years since Conshohocken featured a wrestling event at the Conshohocken A Field located at Eleventh Avenue and Harry Street. The 1958 event featured the Graham Brothers, Dr. Jerry and Ed, and the team of Kid Fox and Chief Big Heart.

EVERY OTHER SPORT

Maddy Crippen, a Conshohocken native, swam nationally for 12 years and won two national championships in the 400-meter individual medley and one in the 200-meter breaststroke. Crippen was a six-year member of the national team, a member of the 1998 and 2003 world championship team, and a member of the 1997, 1999, and 2003 Pan Pacific teams. Conshohocken's only Olympian, she participated in the 2000 Summer Olympics and finished sixth in the 400-meter individual medley. Crippen sits on the Athlete Advisory Committee to the U.S. Olympic Committee. (Courtesy of the Crippen family.)

Dave Traill was a superstar of the Philadelphia Swimming Club and consistently shattered swimming records. Home meets were held in the Miquon section of the Schuylkill River. Traill was also a talented pitcher for a number of baseball teams in the 1920s and 1930s and played semiprofessional baseball and basketball. He later served in the U.S. Navy and was in charge of athletics at the academy. In this 1930 photograph, Traill shows off a few of his swimming trophies.

Conshohocken resident and golf professional John J. Kelly demonstrates how to drive a golf ball out of the water, or perhaps is just cooling off his feet in the mid-1940s at Marble Hall Golf Course. Kelly was appointed as golf professional in the spring of 1942 at Marble Hall after serving a nine-year stint as a caddie. He succeeded Johnny Griffin as the professional. Kelly was the first native-born Conshohocken golfer to compete in a National Open tournament held in Chicago in June 1942.

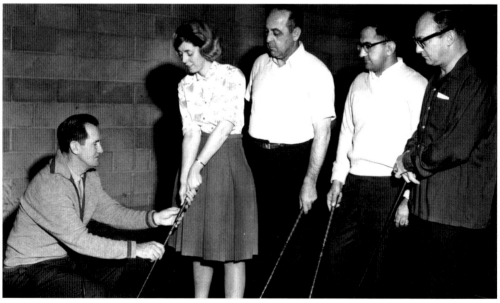

More than 400 golfers attended a free clinic at the Conshohocken Fellowship House in 1962. Kelly, on the left, was a well-known golf professional, and in 1962, Kelly worked at the Oak Terrace Country Club and led the clinic with demonstrations and lectured on the finer points of the game. The pupils are, from left to right, Terry Osta Powicz, Humbert DeStefano, Arthur LaCourse, and Merill Adams.

EVERY OTHER SPORT

Johnny Paul, the greatest bowler from Conshohocken, rolled a 298 in league play at the age of 22 at Charlie Lutter's Conshohocken Community Center Bowling Alleys, once located at Second and Fayette Streets. The American Bowling Congress recognized Paul for rolling three perfect games in league competition. He attracted national attention at a tournament in Detroit and beat a number of the nation's top bowlers. Paul was inducted into the Conshohocken Sports Hall of Fame in 1983. (Courtesy of Patty Paul.)

The John Elwood Lee Surgical Supply Company bowling team from Conshohocken participated in the Philadelphia Wholesale Drug League for many years. The team, far better than any other team in the league, had a slight advantage: Lee owned his own bowling alleys above his carriage house on Forrest Street. Team members in this 1908 photograph are, from left to right, (first row) John Elwood Lee, Charles Herron, and Sam Wright; (second row) Maurice Hallowell and James Wells.

The CBC was built on West Third Avenue in 1929, and bocce teams have been a major part of the organization for many years. In the 1940s and 1950s, the teams representing the club won many local and county championships, once again showing the diversity of Conshohocken sports.

The YMAA of Conshohocken tug-of-war team pulled its way to four straight championships in the early 1900s. Tug-of-war teams were popular because the game was an Olympic sport from 1900 to 1920. Conshohocken won the county title from 1907 to 1910. Members of the team pictured are, from left to right, John Fitzgerald (manager), John "Ace" Reilly, James McDade, Joseph Kelly, and "Big Phil." The photograph was taken outside the YMAA building that formerly served the borough as the first schoolhouse.

EVERY OTHER SPORT

The 39th annual Grand American Trap Shooting Tournament, held in Ohio in 1938, fielded more than 900 marksmen from 40 states. Conshohocken, with members from the Conshohocken Trap-Shooters Gun Club, was the only town to be represented by more than one shooter; Walt Beaver, John Riggs, and Charles Todd all represented the borough. Beaver led all shooters, breaking 198 out of a possible 200 targets; Riggs and Todd followed with 197. Riggs and Beaver set national records over the years and collected many awards. In 1939, at a meet in New Jersey, Riggs broke 397 targets out of a possible 400, setting a national record, and in 1949, Beaver won the 200-bird match, hitting 198 of them and beating more than 873 other marksmen in the annual Delaware State Shoot. The first two men in the photograph from left are unidentified, in the center is Charles Todd, next to him is Walt Beaver, and John Riggs is on the right. This photograph was taken at the Grand American Trap Shooting Tournament held in Ohio in 1938.

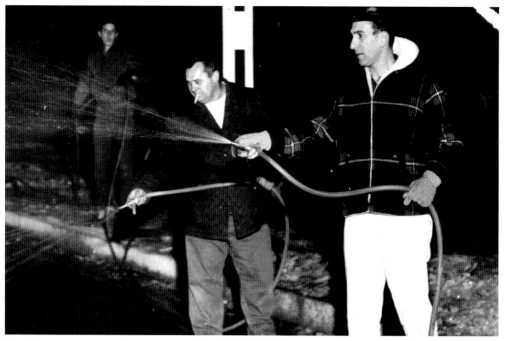

Ice-skating was a popular pastime at Conshohocken's Sutcliffe Park in the early 1960s. Shown above, spraying water for the ice to form on the basketball courts at the playground, are John Gardocki (left), a maintenance supervisor at the park, and Stephen Sirchio. Below, a group of Conshohocken skaters warm their hands and feet at a bonfire built alongside the skating ring.

EVERY OTHER SPORT

Conshohocken High School cheerleaders pose for this picture outside the high school in 1945. The Conshohocken public school system was established on May 15, 1850, the day of the borough's incorporation. Conshohocken High School, once located on the corner of West Seventh Avenue and Fayette Street, was built in 1913 and closed in the spring of 1966. Posing are, from left to right, Marie Hall, Jeanne Beaver, Nadaio DiPetro (the male standing in the back), Jean Alleva, Mary Jane Gilbert, and Christine Fabrize.

When the Conshohocken midget football program was formed in 1961, cheerleaders became a part of the program in the inaugural year. In 1979, these girls cheered the 100-pound team on to victory. Members of the team include Paulette Champagne, Cynthia Gredius, Joan Komorowski, Erica Scott, Cathy Ellis, Cindy Lesniewski, and Michele Martinelli.

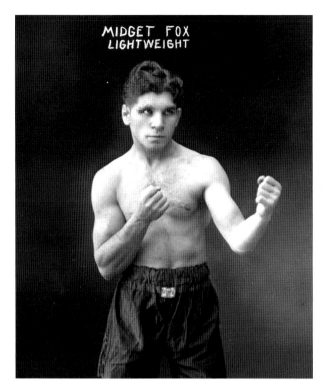

MIDGET FOX
LIGHTWEIGHT

Among Conshohocken's greatest boxers is Anthony Rossi, known in the boxing world as Midget Fox. In his heyday, Fox lived on East Hector Street and fought 108 professional fights in the lightweight and featherweight divisions. He fought in the tristate area and recorded 61 victories, 25 losses, and 9 draws. Fox stands at the top of the list with other boxers like Johnny Craven, Joey Hatfield, Joey Blake, Kid Silvers, and Jesse Zadroga.

The Hamilton Paper Company's bowling team from the mid-1930s was part of the Conshohocken Industrial Classic Bowling League that participated in league play for more than 40 years. The well-dressed Hamilton team was led by Jimmy Traill; notice all the bowlers wore their name on their tie. The paper company, located in the Miquon section of Whitemarsh Township, employed thousands of Conshohocken residents.

Conshohocken native Fred DeStolfo started studying the sport of tae kwon do in 1971 and by 1977 opened DeStolfo's Premier Martial Arts, which continues today. DeStolfo is a seventh-degree black belt in tae kwon do. He presides as the United States eastern regional director of the International Chin Mu Kwan Tae Kwon Do Federation, supervising training and promotion of black belts in the region. In 1988, DeStolfo was inducted into the International Karate Hall of Fame.

Johnny Hannon, from Morristown, was a 26-year-old dirt track race car champion in Norristown. He worked on his cars at Galie's Garage in the Connaughtown section of Conshohocken. In 1934, he became the AAA Eastern Circuit champion and earned a trip to the 1935 Indianapolis 500. He drove high into the third turn at Indianapolis on his first qualifying round, skidded across the track through a concrete retaining wall, and was killed instantly. Hannon was inducted into the National Sprint Car Hall of Fame in 2006 at the 17th annual induction ceremonies.

Conshohocken boxer Johnny Craven, born Casimer Grablewski, won 62 fights as an amateur before going professional. As a professional, Craven fought 140 fights, winning 128, with 44 knockouts; he lost 5 fights by decision and 2 by technical knockouts, and he had 5 draws. All seven of the fights he lost he won in a rematch. Craven started his professional career in 1930 by winning 30 straight fights, 7 by decision and 23 by knockouts, after losing a fight to Joe Figlietto, whom he defeated in a rematch. He then ran his record to 55-1. Craven retired several times to open a diner and the Square Circle Tavern in Conshohocken.

The Archbishop Kennedy High School football team was recognized for an undefeated football season at the annual Conshohocken Sports Hall of Fame induction ceremonies in 1981. From left to right are Bill Collins, founder and director of the hall of fame; Chris Bockrath, head coach of the Archbishop Kennedy High School undefeated football team (11-0); Joseph Connely and George Rafferty, both directors of the hall of fame; and Chuck Leheam, athletic director for the high school.

In December 1991, a group of former standout athletes gathered at the Great American Pub located on Fayette Street to reminisce about their glory days. Pictured are, from left to right, (first row) Bob Behacy, Burr Robbins, George Pettine, Whitey Mellor, Sunny Garvey, and Andy Kane; (second row) Totsie Stybinski, Dan O'Donnell, George Snear, Lou DiGiacomo, Bud Reiley, and Mick McGuigan.

The Conshohocken Sports Hall of Fame, founded in 1978, was one of the first local halls of fame in Montgomery County and the Philadelphia area. Dignitaries and inductees pose for this photograph in 1983 at the fifth annual induction ceremonies. Standing are, from left to right, Michael Ethridge, John Maloney, Joseph Golas, Harry "Butch" Kitt, Herb Magee (guest speaker), John Paul (great bowler), John "Chick" McCarter (sports historian), Ed Swift, William O'Donnell, Michael O'Rourke, and Michael Pettine.

Frank Zoltowski, left, presents Art "Tuti" Andrey with an award at the 1985 annual St. Matthew's CYO banquet. Zoltowski, a director with the CYO program for many years and a longtime employee of the Conshohocken Fellowship House, honored Andrey for his many hours of volunteerism not only to the CYO but also with all of Conshohocken's youth programs, including Little League baseball. Zoltowski was a 2008 inductee into the Montgomery County Coaches Hall of Fame.

Starting in 1922, Philadelphia A's owner Connie Mack would play a Sunday game every summer at the Spring Mill Country Club, once located on the corner of North Lane and East Hector Street. The A's would play local teams like Villanova University or the Philadelphia Electric team. In 1930, Mack showed off his starting infield with, from left to right, hall of famer Jimmy Foxx, ? Bishop, ? Boley, and the great Jimmy Dykes. Thousands of Conshohocken residents would crowd the fence to get a glimpse of their favorite players.

6

FELLOWSHIP HOUSE

This was a typical scene at the front doors of the Fellowship House on the first day of registration for after-school programs in the early 1960s. It was common for more than 1,000 youngsters to register on the first day after school every fall. Joan Welcher, sitting at right, registers the children. Standing at the far left is Connie Howell, one of the activity leaders at the time, and next to her is Albert C. Donofrio, the Fellowship House's executive director from 1959 to 1976.

John Sabia, chairman of D. M. Sabia of Conshohocken, addresses a crowd gathered at the Fellowship House revitalization kickoff program held in 2000. Sabia discussed the need for expansion and served on the advisory committee for the $3 million project. Sabia, who has since passed away, contributed to many of Conshohocken's projects and youth programs for decades. In February 2004, the new Fellowship House was dedicated with a mission to provide recreation and education service opportunities for all Conshohocken citizens.

Nearly five years of planning and construction led to a $3 million renovation to the Fellowship House. In 2004, a grand opening was held to dedicate the renovation and expansion of the Fellowship House. Members of the board of directors overseeing the project are, from left to right, Craig Hunter, Peter Moore, Mark Viggiano, Dale Malentonio, Dave Minnick, Margaret Cassidy, Ray Staley, Joe Kelly, George Snear, Marie McMonagle, Lucius Carter, and Jack Coll.

The game of soccer was played a little different in the early 1960s at the Fellowship House. Girls from Harvey Walker Elementary School and St. Matthew's Grade School can be seen playing the game in their dresses and loafers.

During the first 10 to 12 years at the Fellowship House (founded in 1953), plays and stage shows were common in the main gymnasium area, as seen by the actors in this undated photograph from the early 1960s. Albert C. Donofrio took over as the Fellowship House director in 1959 and encouraged stage shows and expanded the youth center's programs, attracting more than 2,000 registered area children per year to the facility.

Children enjoy after-school activities in this late-1950s photograph in the Fellowship House all-purpose room. Fellowship House director William S. Leedale established a good program foundation in his five years as director (1954–1959). A few of Leedale's activities included tap dancing classes, ballroom dancing, baton twirling, charm and self-improvement classes, dog obedience class, and storytelling, just to name a few.

The most talked about activity of the Fellowship House over the years was, and is, kickball. Everyone was a hero for a game, as they kicked the winning run or put the ball up on the balcony for a home run. The young boys seen in this early-1960s kickball game are now parents and grandparents.

The Fellowship House has been promoting sports and solid community programs since 1953 from its Fifth Avenue and Harry Street location. Winning trophies at the Fellowship House in the early 1960s was a big deal for children. Posing are members of the fifth-grade championship basketball team, from left to right, (first row) Tom Deuber, Jim Groves, Bob Omar, and Mike Hatfield; (second row) Mike Cantu, Stan Pearson, Bill Racich, John Ellam, and Tom Roberts.

The after-school arts-and-crafts class was always popular throughout the 1950s and 1960s, as was the doll-making class. This was just one of many supervised activities that were part of the early Fellowship House schedule. Adult classes included hat making, lamp shade making, and dog grooming.

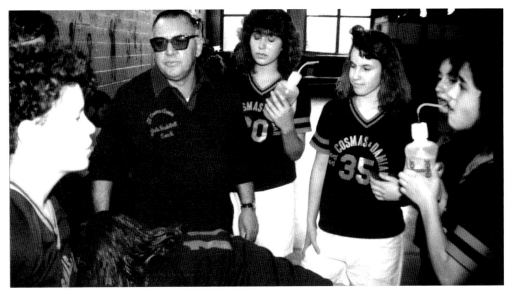

Don Stemple, head coach of the SS. Cosmas and Damian CYO girls' basketball, takes a time-out during a game in 1989 at the Fellowship House. Stemple was a basketball coach in Conshohocken and West Conshohocken for more than four decades, coaching every level of boys' and girls' basketball. Stemple coached teams in the early Conshohocken Teenage Basketball Classic tournament in the early 1960s; he also coached teams in West Conshohocken and St. Gertrude's CYO.

This group of youngsters from the mid-1980s takes time out during a pool game at the Fellowship House to pose for a photograph. In recent years, the youth center has increased sports and educational programs but still offers games like pool and Ping-Pong.

Christmas is always a happy and celebrated time at the Fellowship House, as it was in 1986 when these CYO youngsters gathered for a picture in front of the Christmas tree. In the photograph above, the young ladies put the finishing touches on the Christmas tree just before the annual dance party. They are, from left to right, 12-year-old Megan Gebhardt, 10-year-old Nora Hass, and 9-year-old Tara Leonard. In the photograph below, Fellowship House supervisor Jimmy Moore helps children decorate the Christmas tree.

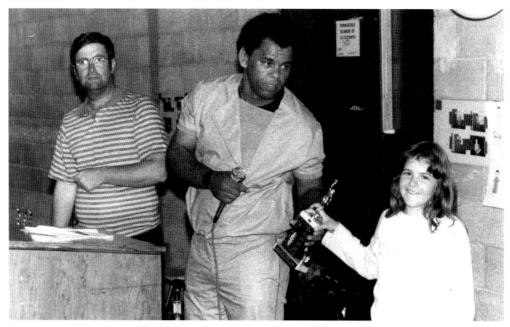

In 1991, Darlene Hildebrand accepts a trophy at the annual St. Matthew's CYO banquet, held at the Fellowship House each year. Her coaches, Frank Zoltowski on the left and Jimmy Moore in the middle, present her with her award. Hildebrand was a junior varsity player back then and went on to set all kinds of records at Archbishop Kennedy High School and Philadelphia Textile College. Hildebrand is currently the executive director at the Fellowship House.

In the early 1960s, the Fellowship House was a winter workout conditioning facility for several Major League Baseball players, including Bobby Shantz, Al Spangler, Jack Sanford, and Curt Simmons. Shantz, a longtime pitcher for the Philadelphia A's, also played for the Pittsburgh Pirates and the Houston Colts. Sanford, seen holding the baseball bat, was the ace pitcher for the San Francisco Giants for many years. Shantz's son Teddy is seen on the far left next to his dad, and Johnny Sanford is on the right.

Christmas has always been a great time of year at the Fellowship House. Children of all ages get to visit with Santa, and every child receives a gift. Christmas parties and CYO events have always added to the festivities of the holiday.

The Fellowship House has provided many activities since it opened in 1953, and in the early 1960s, ice-skating was one of the more popular activities. Shown ice-skating at Sutcliffe Park are, from left to right, Kathy McGrath, Marie Bono, Pat DiGregario, Leona Burt, and Kathy Januzelli.

Ice-skating was a very popular winter activity for many years in many communities throughout the 1960s. Conshohocken was one of the communities that ran ice-skating events on outdoor basketball courts. Ice-skating at Sutcliffe Park was sponsored by the Fellowship House from 1960 to 1966. These three youngsters skating at Sutcliffe Park seem to be having a good time; notice the two children on the left favor the old strap-on ice-skates.

Albert C. Donofrio, executive director of the Fellowship House, was the force behind ice-skating in Conshohocken. In 1960, the Fellowship House arranged to have the basketball courts at Sutcliffe Park frozen for ice-skating; typically about 300 residents would show up to skate. These young ladies having a grand old time on the ice are, from left to right, Noreen Carson, Maryanne Pasquini, Margie Verruni, and Anita Farini.

FELLOWSHIP HOUSE

BASKETBALL

While the Conshohocken Pioneers had a very successful season in 1896–1897, when this photograph was taken, they managed to lose a game to the Trenton Athletic Club by a score of 2-0. The game was played in full but only one shot fell from half court. However, the Pioneers won a game 22-0 over the Caledonian squad. The seven members of the squad include William Neville, Bob Crawford, Billy Bennett, Frank Moore, ? Cox, ? Ruth, and ? Ellam.

Conshohocken's YMAA second team poses for a team photograph in the spring of 1901. While players like Bulger, Murphy, and Huzzard played on the YMAA first team, it was common back in the day for the team's second unit to hold its own schedule, as did this young group composed of George Rafferty, Edmond Rafferty, Jim McDade, John Rielly, Hayes, McDade, Messimer, and team manager Ed Lightham.

The Conshohocken professional basketball team of 1904–1905, known as the Giants, recorded a 32-8 record. This photograph of professional basketball's first world champions hangs in the Naismith Memorial Basketball Hall of Fame. The team led the league in scoring with 1,548 points, with Steve White, Bill Keenan, Charles Bossert, and Allen Glassey among the top 12 scorers in the league. From left to right are (first row) team mascot Johnny O'Keefe; (second row) Bill Keenan, Steve White, Bill Herron, Charles Bossert, and Allen Glassey; (third row) Ed Leightham, Billy Bennet, George Huzzard, and Billy Neville.

BASKETBALL

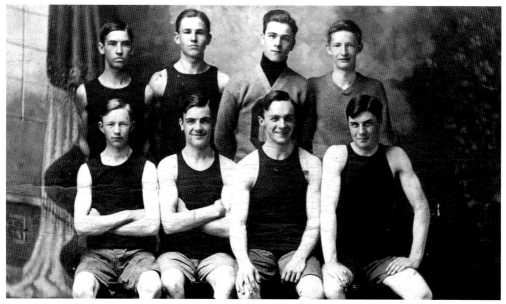

Basketball was a much different sport in the early part of last century. The Conshohocken High School Basketball Club played teams like North Wales, East End (Norristown), Reliance (West Conshohocken), and North Philadelphia. Several members of the team included Wesley, Hayes, Murphy, Lacy, and Fitzgerald.

The 1911 West Conshohocken Reliance basketball team won the league and county championships after beating teams from throughout Montgomery County and Philadelphia. Harry Ellam and John Clinton (neither appear in this photograph) proved to be the team's heavy scorers, and Ellam was a pillar at his center position. Pictured are, from left to right, (first row) Howard "Chitcher" Armitage, Roy Ramey (captain), and Joe Connelly; (second row) Frank Herron, Ed Hyde (player-manager), and Billy McCabe.

The championship basketball team of the Conshohocken Boys Club from 1911 to 1912 posted a 12-3 record, losing only one game at home. Team members, made up of young men from First Baptist Church, included Eisenberg, who led the team in scoring with 143 points for the year, just ahead of Merkle, who scored 141 points. Other team members included Grennor, Sweimler, Lewis, J. Riker, and N. Riker. Perhaps the biggest victory of the season was over crosstown (cross-street) rivals St. Mark's, with a 33-22 victory.

This Conshohocken High School girls' team in 1915 and 1916 played when only the two forwards could shoot the ball and the guards had to remain beyond the half-court line. The Conshohocken Lassies finished the season with a 4-4 record, including a 40-12 loss to Lansdale, but finished with a 49-9 victory over Norristown. From left to right are (first row) Reba Balmer, Esther Ferrier, and Mary Albright; (second row) Margaret Murray and Elizabeth Raysor.

BASKETBALL

The Conshohocken High School boys' basketball team of 1917–1918 went undefeated, posting the school's first perfect record in sports. William Davis, Charles Irwin, and Johnny McBride helped the team score 754 points while winning 15 games. Members of the team seen here are, from left to right, (first row) George Nyce, Charles Miller, and Austin Davies; (second row) Charles Irwin, Johnny McBride, William Davis, and George Beaver; (third row) William "Pop" Irwin (coach), Carl Nagle (manager), and John Falkenstine.

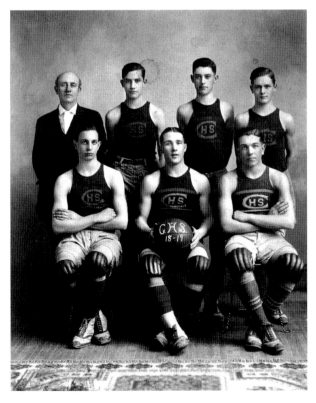

The Conshohocken High School boys' basketball team was undefeated during the 1918–1919 season, posting 21 victories. The team's two biggest victories came over Souderton, with a 60-9 win, and over Quakertown, with an unheard of score of 94-30. From left to right are (first row) George Beaver, Johnny McBride, and Harry Merkel; (second row) Pop Irwin (coach), Charles Irwin, William Bate, and Ralph Wentling.

Conshohocken High School girls' basketball was very successful in the school's early years. Formed in 1915, the girls' team had winning seasons for nearly a decade. In 1919–1920, the girls lost only one game, followed by an undefeated season in 1920–1921 and a championship season in 1921–1922, posting a 13-1 record. Pop Irwin stands behind his 1919–1920 team along with, in no particular order, Polly Wood, Dorothy Davis, Jane Warrell, Murl Harrold, Molly Ferrier, Mabel Doughtery, Dorothy Hiltner, and Ella Fairlie.

The 1921 boys' basketball team from Conshohocken High School capped off a very successful season beating Jenkintown High School 31-29 in overtime. Seen here are, from left to right, (first row) Charlie Head, Ralph Wentling, and Sam Bresen (who lived above his father's tailor shop next to Baldwin Flowers); (second row) Bill Irwin (the coach's son), Bill Jones, Tubey Freas, Everett Thompson (an all-state track runner), Jim Ronnon, and Pop Irwin (coach).

BASKETBALL

The Conshohocken High School girls' basketball team of 1928–1929 won the lower Montgomery County championship in the spring of 1929. The lady cagers beat Bridgeport 23-11 to seal an undefeated season. Members of the team are, from left to right, (first row) Jessie Gravell, Kathryn Smith, Polly Faust, Alice Schlichter, and Ruth Ramsey; (second row) Margaret Glass, Helen Eisenberg, Marion Davidson, Lena Carl (coach), unidentified, and Ruth Auerback.

From 1928 to 1929, this team won the lower section of Montgomery County League. While not all the members on the team are identified, the ones that are include F. Fairlie, S. Webster, Winterbottom, K. Heist, H. Gibson, V. Bonkoski, P. Smith, M. Limbert, J. Vangeriff, Johnstone, E. Love, B. Fairlie, J. DelBuno, Godshalk, and Lentz. In the back row are D. Tees (manager) and R. Grimmett (coach).

In 1930, the Baptist team won its third straight championship in the Conshohocken Church League. The team would go on to win five consecutive championships from 1928 to 1932. The four Irwin brothers dominated the games, with Jack and Ed scoring most of the team's points. Members of the team included Jack, Ed, Bill, and Spike Irwin; Tony Holden; Chief Murray, Sam Knight; ? Logan; and ? Risley. Church league games were played at the Red Men's Hall, located at Sixth Avenue and Harry Street, and drew more than 200 spectators per game.

Members of the 1929–1930 Knights of Columbus team, champions of the Schuylkill Valley Basketball League, pose for a photograph following the championship game. From left to right are (first row) Phillip Gardocki, Ernest Pettine, James Pettine (captain), James Mellon, and George Chmielewski; (second row) Charles Millhouse and Joseph Carolin; (third row) Edward A. Fitzgerald (secretary and treasurer), Edward A. O'Brien (manager), Rev. Thomas Peleshek (director), Leo Redmond, and Edmund Hurley (grand knight).

BASKETBALL

During the 1920s and 1930s, basketball was the only competitive sport for females at Conshohocken High School. During those early years, the school fielded some very good teams, including the 1930–1931 team. The team enjoyed big victories over Berwyn, Springfield, and Cheltenham.

Conshohocken High School's 1933–1934 basketball team had a number of the school's most talented athletes to ever run the courts in the high school's history. The team had a good year, finishing tied for second place with Lansdowne. Seen here are, from left to right, (first row) Art Ramsay, Chot Wood, Jacob Feingold, John Rumpton, and Whitey Mellor; (second row) Nick DiCamillo, George Pulman, Russ Grimmett, and George Feingold.

The 1941 Conshohocken High School boys' basketball team won a league championship with its 12-4 season record. The highlight of the season was a 33-14 victory over Bridgeport and a pair of victories over West Conshohocken. Team members include, from left to right, (first row) Sztubinski, Zajac, Zajac, Hylinski, and Sztubinski; (second row) Zoltowski, Bate, Tees, Opelski, and O'Donnell; (third row) coaches Dougherty, Fox, and Januzelli.

In 1940, the Conshohocken High School boys' basketball team finished with a 9-9 record, winning five of its nine games by two points. Pictured are, from left to right, (first row) Tees, Bate, Butera, Kurylek, Jacobs, and Sztubinski; (second row) Zajac, Opelski, Shaw, coach Harry Fox, Zajac, and Dutill; (third row) O'Donell, Sztubinski, Hylinski, Ochnich, Zoltowski, Shaw, and Grabeck; (fourth row) Januzelli, Smith, Ristine, Elmo, Heleniek, DeWalt, and Doughtery.

BASKETBALL

In the late 1940s, former students and athletes of Conshohocken and St. Matthew's High Schools came together to become part of the Corsairs Boys Club. The Corsairs Boys Club sponsored baseball and basketball teams in local leagues and was a mainstay in Conshohocken civic basketball leagues for many years. Seen here are, from left to right, (first row) Joe Leddy, Joe Mashett, and Bob Ehlenger; (second row) Lou Cappelli, Ed Czarnecki, George Snear, Joe Purcell, and Joe Martinelli. (Courtesy of Bob Ehlenger.)

In the spring of 1941, the West Conshohocken High School basketball team celebrated a Suburban Six PIAA championship. The team recorded a 14-5 record including a one-point victory over Upper Merion 22-21. Members of the team include, from left to right, (first row) John Huber (manager), Frank Diesinger, Leo Prusinowski, Robert McDonnell, Ed Fenelon, and Paul Swartz (manager); (second row) William Hilt, Jack Hinchey (coach), Robert Schrack, Fred Ingram, William Schaffer, Francis Kennedy, and Jack Graham. Robert and Albert Slater were not present for the photograph.

In 1941, members of the Conshohocken Hy Club were champions of the Philadelphia Suburban Main Line League; they also won a championship in the Norristown League that same year. Seen here are, from left to right, (first row) Dan O'Donnell, Slim Paulkner, Whitey Mellor, Knute Lawler, and Chot Wood; (second row) George Pettine, Elwood Heller, Ed Wood, Sammy Webster, and Tinker Rowan.

The 1942 Conshohocken High School boys' basketball team had quite a season, winning the Suburban Six championship. The team posted a 13-1 regular-season record, averaging 40 points per game. Members of the team included Fox, Pasquinni, Murray, Novi, DeWalt, Kasopsky, Rodenbaugh, Shaw, Grabeck, Zoltowski, Zajac, Stubinski, Hylinski, and O'Donnell.

BASKETBALL

In the spring of 1964, the Conshohocken High School boys' basketball team won the PIAA Class C basketball championship. It was a great moment in the school's history and a proud moment for all Conshohocken residents. In the photograph above, members of the championship team celebrate while riding atop a Washington Fire Company truck in a parade on Fayette Street that lasted for hours.

In the spring of 1964, the Conshohocken High School basketball team posted a 15-3 regular season record and a 4-0 playoff record that won it a state championship; the final game was a 63-48 victory over Coudersport. In the photograph above are, from left to right, (first row) Ernie Mathis, Harry Kitt, Thomas White, Robert Graham, and Adam Ciccotti; (second row) Michael DePalma, Michael Howell, Mike Etheridge, and Joe McFadden; (third row) Francis Omar and John Ruben. In the photograph below, five of the Class C champions gather when the Conshohocken Sports Hall of Fame honored the team. From left to right are John Ruben, Michael DePalma, Thomas White, Michael Howell, and Ernie Mathis.

DONOFRIO BASKETBALL

The late beloved Albert C. Donofrio of Conshohocken passed away on July 4, 1976. Donofrio graduated from Bridgeport High School in 1950 and was a standout in several sports. By 1959, Donofrio was an assistant director at the Fellowship House, before being named director in December of that year. Over the next 16 years, Donofrio built bridges and friendships. As a lasting tribute, the Conshohocken Teenage Basketball Classic tournament that he founded in 1960 was renamed the Albert C. Donofrio Basketball Tournament, referred to hereafter as the Donofrio tournament.

Earl Monroe, on the left, poses with John Anderson when the two were teammates at John Bartram High School. Before playing at Winston-Salem State University, Monroe played in the Conshohocken Teenage Basketball Classic (referred to as the tournament) at the Fellowship House in 1962. He went on to play professional basketball with the Baltimore Bullets and the New York Knicks from 1967 until he retired in 1980. Monroe was known throughout his career as "the Pearl," "Black Magic," and "Black Jesus." He was a 1990 inductee into the Naismith Memorial Basketball Hall of Fame.

In 1963, the Purcell team lost a thriller to Technical Maintenance 67-66, as Mellor's Sporting Goods went on to win the championship that year. Members of the J. P. Purcell team are, from left to right, (first row) J. Farrell, M. Forrester, and J. Turk; (second row) J. Farrell, A. Enoch, W. McGarritty, and head coach Don Stemple.

In 1963, the Fellowship House was one of the best high school basketball tournaments in the Philadelphia area. Mellor's Sporting Goods won the third annual tournament in a come-from-behind victory, 81-71, over Ray's Tavern. From left to right are (first row) J. Troilio, T. McPhearson, L. Moman, and M. McDaniel; (second row) R. Klein (manager), R. Nelson, W. Smith, and G. Smith. Fred Carter scored eight points for Ray's Tavern in a losing effort, but Carter went on to coach the Philadelphia 76ers for several years in the late 1990s.

Members of Mellor's Sporting Goods pose for a team picture after winning their second straight championship in 1964. Pictured here showing off the trophy in the first row are, from left to right, Whitey Mellor (sponsor), Dick Kline (coach), Bobby Mellor, Joe Heiser, and Carl Aumann (trophy donor and one-time owner of Carl's Diner, at Fourth Avenue and Fayette Street). Among those in the second row are Bob Brooker, Earl Williams, Rich Berberian, Dick Tyler, Mike Kempski, Maurice Savage, Pete Straup, and Bobby Lewis.

Ray's Tavern was knocked out of the tournament early in 1964, losing to Town Valet in a heartbreaker 93-91. Seen here are, from left to right, (first row) Andy Toth, Cliff Risell, Ed Davis, Harry Kitt, Herb Brown, and Tom Sierzega; (second row) John Mahoney, J. B. Sanders (manager), Mike Etheridge, Jack Bryant, Sid Hawks, Walt Davis, and D. Amarusa (manager).

This photograph from the 1964 tournament may have been titled "All Eyes on the Ball," as members from National Paint and J. P. Purcell battle for the ball. Grabbing for the ball is National Paint's Hal Booker, while J. P. Purcell's Jim Farrell gets a hand in. Looking on in the center are Mike Barrett of J. P. Purcell and Ed Szczesny of National Paint. National Paint won the game 105-96.

In the spring of 1964, the fourth annual tournament was played at the Conshohocken Fellowship House, and when it was all over, Mellor's Sporting Goods had won the championship and National Paint was the runner-up. Posing with trophies are, from left to right, Rich Berberian from West Catholic High School, who won the sportsmanship award; Bob Brooker from Simon Gratz High School, who was named co-MVP; and Rich Cornwall from Neshaminy High School, who was also co-MVP.

Typical game action at the 1965 tournament held at the Conshohocken Fellowship House shows Ken Shamberger of National Paint tapping in a shot over Town Valet's Wayne Betz. To the left of the play, hoping for a rebound, is National Paint's Buddy Harris, while other players at right look on. The players at right include Vern Fisher, Al Laughinghouse, and "Hoss" Zielinski.

While Ray's Tavern had some talented players on the team in 1965, it was knocked out of the tournament at the Fellowship House. In 1965, Ray's lost to Mellor's Sporting Goods and Mirabile Beverage. From left to right are (first row) unidentified; (second row) T. Michell, J. Sivick, C. Persley, B. Baer, E. Smith, B. New, and J. Elvin; (third row) R. New (coach), J. Tracey, G. Smith, J. Reuben, R. Breski, R. Engles, J. Sodowski, M. Thornton, J. Harper, D. Klinebach, and Ray Gravinese (sponsor).

Don Stemple, standing on the left, was the head basketball coach of the J. P. Purcell basketball team in 1966 at the sixth annual tournament. The tournament has attracted big-name players from six different states over the years. Seen here are, from left to right, (first row) J. Leukowicz, T. Czerpak, J. Harper, B. Biernbaum, and M. O'Rourke; (second row) coach Don Stemple, F. McLaughlin, E. Linker, C. Strunk, S. Schafer, and S. Newman.

The Chapel Pharmacy basketball team had some very talented players in 1967, including John Lewkowicz, Chuck Eckman, Bill Bovell, and John Leonard. Chapel Pharmacy won a couple of games, including a 74-72 upset victory over the Upstarters, before being bounced from the 1967 tournament. Seen here are, from left to right, (first row) J. Schaeffer, R. Holland, J. Lewkowicz, J. Leonard, and W. Bovell; (second row) J. Lewkowicz, R. Redcay, C. Eckman, P. Harubin, M. Grimes, L. Athens, and M. Mullett.

In 1970, Chris Aumann presents the championship trophy at the 10th annual tournament held at the Fellowship House. The Carl Aumann Memorial Trophy was presented to Green's Pharmacy of Bridgeport after defeating McGovern Enterprises 93-85. Standing are, from left to right, Bill Brennen, team sponsor; Jim Huggard, coach; Chris Aumann, who was the daughter of the late Carl Aumann; Tony Samartino, coach; and Albert C. Donofrio, tournament director.

Impressive hardware was handed out in 1970 upon the completion of the 10th annual tournament at the Fellowship House. MVP awards were presented by Albert C. Donofrio, on the left, to Steve Joachim of McGovern Enterprises and Jim O'Brien of Green's Pharmacy. On the far right is Tom Jordan, also of Green's Pharmacy, who was presented the sportsmanship trophy. Green's Pharmacy won the tournament 93-85 over McGovern Enterprises.

In the late 1960s and early 1970s, Henry Williams played basketball for Norristown High School and was one of the best basketball players to ever play in Montgomery County. Williams is seen here playing at the Fellowship House in the 1971 for the Salvation Army team. Williams is showing off his ballhandling skills during a game with Green's Pharmacy; Green's Pharmacy topped the Salvation Army 99-86 despite Williams's fine play. Behind Williams is Green's Pharmacy's Fran Rafferty, and on the right is his Salvation Army teammate Larry Mills.

It was Albert C. Donofrio's pleasure to present the championship trophy to the owners of Quaker Tire, who won the championship in 1972. Accepting the championship trophy from Donofrio, tournament and Fellowship House director, following a 104-98 victory over McGovern Enterprises are Tom Thornton (second from left) and Bob Gallop, owners of Quaker Tire. Andy McGovern (right), coach of McGovern Enterprises, is accepting the runner-up trophy.

The Fellowship House has a small court with limited seating, and on most nights of the three-week-long Donofrio tournament, the gymnasium plays to standing-room crowds only. Spectators on the right with their feet hanging out over the playing line include Lionel Simmons (first row, fourth from right), a LaSalle standout in the late 1980s before playing in the NBA. Simmons is seen checking out a game between Sonny Hill and the Roadrunners in 1990.

Donofrio tournament announcers and scorekeepers have come and gone, but three familiar faces include, from left to right, Frank Zoltowski, who has worked all the tournaments to date and kept the score books for more than 20 years; Kevin Hollingsworth, an announcer for many years; and Don Stemple, who coached several teams in the early years and ran the scoreboard for 30 years at the tournaments. This photograph was taken in 1990 during the 30th anniversary of the tournament.

In 1993, Jim Donofrio coached the Don-Len basketball team at the annual Donofrio tournament. Jim's father, Albert C., was the director at the Fellowship House from 1959 until his death in 1976. The tournament draws 24 teams a year for the three-week-long event. Many of the players on their way to the NBA have participated in the tournament, such as Earl "the Pearl" Monroe, Aaron McKie, Joe Bryant and his son Kobe Bryant, Rasheed Wallace, Fred Carter, Lionel Simmons, Gene Banks, John Salmons, Geoff Petrie, and Matt Goukas.

Wallace was a 6-foot-11-inch All-America center from Gratz High School who played in the Donofrio tournament for three years. In the image above, Wallace takes in some music and enjoys the company of some local Conshohocken youths. At right, Wallace pushes down one of his many slam-dunks at the Fellowship House in 1993 as he led his HBA Point Breeze team to a 116-57 victory. Wallace had signed with North Carolina and has played for more than a decade in the NBA.

Joe "Jellybean" Bryant, on the left, poses with his son Kobe in 1996 when Kobe played the Donofrio tournament at the Conshohocken Fellowship House. Both Joe and Kobe played the Fellowship House tournament and both played professional basketball. Kobe, No. 21 in the front row, poses below with the rest of the Sonny Hill Juniors who won the Donofrio championship in 1996.

The only time during the first 49 years of the Donofrio tournament that a father and son both captured the MVP award was by Joe and Kobe Bryant. Joe actually won two MVP awards in 1971 and is shown in the photograph above in 1972. He poses with Mike Sojurner, far left, who won the sportsmanship award; co-MVP Mo Howard, far right; and tournament director Albert C. Donofrio, second from right, who presents the trophy. Joe later enjoyed a career in the NBA. In the photograph below, George Snear, on the left, a member of the board of directors at the Fellowship House, helps Floyd Schaffer, Fellowship House director, right, present MVP trophies to Donnie Carr of Positive Image and Kobe Bryant of the Sonny Hill Juniors. Kobe, like his father, has enjoyed a long career in the NBA, winning MVP awards and league championships.

Across America, People are Discovering Something Wonderful. *Their Heritage.*

Arcadia Publishing is the leading local history publisher in the United States. With more than 3,000 titles in print and hundreds of new titles released every year, Arcadia has extensive specialized experience chronicling the history of communities and celebrating America's hidden stories, bringing to life the people, places, and events from the past. To discover the history of other communities across the nation, please visit:

www.arcadiapublishing.com

Customized search tools allow you to find regional history books about the town where you grew up, the cities where your friends and family live, the town where your parents met, or even that retirement spot you've been dreaming about.